Office Politics

Office Politics

A survival guide

by

Jane Clarke

First published in 1999 by
The Industrial Society
Robert Hyde House
48 Bryanston Square
London W1H 7LN
Telephone: 0171 479 2000

© Jane Clarke 1999

ISBN 1 85835 532 X

Stylus Publishing Inc.
22883 Quicksilver Drive
Sterling
VA 20166–2012
USA

British Library Cataloguing-in-Publication Data.
A catalogue record for this book is available from the
British Library.

Library of Congress
Cataloguing-in-Publication
Data on File.

Typeset by: The Midlands Book Typesetting Company
Printed by: J W Arrowsmith Ltd
Cover by: Sign Design
Cover image: Images

The Industrial Society is a Registered Charity No. 290003

852tw7.99

Dedication

This book is dedicated to my father, Geoff Clarke, whose experience of corporate life revealed to me the darker side of office politics, and to my sister Sarah, whose pursuit of a politics-free zone at work convinces me that it just can't be done.

Acknowledgements

I would like to express my gratitude to John Nicholson for his priceless input throughout – from initial concept to final edit. Thanks too to Cathy Walton who gave up part of her holiday to make an invaluable contribution, and to the Nicholson McBride Central Services team for their patient research and careful proofing. Finally, I would like to thank those at The Industrial Society for their support and guidance, in particular Susannah Lear, Angela Ishmael and Andrew Forrest.

Contents

Introduction

Office politics gets a very bad press. People sneer at those who engage in it too obviously, and complain of being victimized. But why should this be so, when political activity consists merely of showing an interest outside your immediate ken, and trying to have an influence on events? It could be something to do with the reasons – real or imagined – *behind* the actions. Some people certainly play the office political game for negative reasons – feathering their own nest, for example, rather than trying to progress towards common goals.

Office politicians also approach their "dark art" with varying degrees of competence. Some are able to achieve an enormous amount, and come out the other end squeaky clean, while others only succeed in drawing attention to their inability to achieve their selfish objectives. Finally, there are those people who sit on the sidelines and merely observe the political goings on, unwilling to dirty their own hands. Such people are unlikely to be positive about the results of *Realpolitick* office-style, even when they benefit personally from them.

Psychologists believe that we are born with a desire to understand and to influence what is going on immediately around us. So political activity, following the strict definition given above, is simply a fact of life – in the office, as elsewhere. And it can be a positive thing, when it's focused on steering events for the common good within your circle of influence. This book accepts that it's positive and constructive to have people taking part in political activity – in organizations, as in governments. Otherwise, there is a risk of lack of common direction, isolated teams, and overall fragmentation.

Organized into two parts (Part One looking at the background to office politics, Part Two offering practical advice on handling specific political issues), this then is a handbook for people at all levels who want a better understanding of office politics and how to make things happen.

Of course, there's always a danger of office politics being abused – either deliberately or unknowingly. But if this happens, at least you should be in a position to counter, deal with – or at least be aware of – what's going on. In short, you should become better informed, and better equipped to deal with the jungle of business life.

Part One

CHAPTER 1

What is office politics?

A survey of UK-based executives asked people to outline what office politics meant to them. The responses were very interesting.

Most agreed that it was all about gaining power and exerting influence. It was thought to be the emotional, rather than the rational – the informal, rather than the formal – way of getting things done. People agreed that political activity tends to be focused internally – looking after colleagues' egos – rather than externally – meeting customers' needs. And it's all about pursuing goals – usually the individual's own, rather than those of the organization. The vast majority of respondents stated that politics was something they always had to bear in mind – while a smaller number said it was rife throughout their organization. Fewer than 5% of the respondents felt that politics played little or no part. Since political activity was considered to be so widespread, it was significant that 80% rated office politics as destructive, rather than constructive.

Taken from Office Politics Survey, Nicholson McBride, 1998

Introduction

Manipulating, manoeuvering, string pulling, game playing, backstabbing, bitching, buck-passing, bullying, sucking up, stamping down, claiming success, diverting blame: mention office politics and these are the sorts of phrases that people will use to describe their contempt for the whole shooting match.

Office politics is one of the most talked about dimensions of working life. It's blamed for many of the injustices and wrongdoings we encounter in the workplace. And it's usually something that *other* people do! But it wasn't always that way.

The word "politics" is derived from the ancient Greek word *polis* which means city state – the organizational structure introduced to help create some order in a society with many diverse, and sometimes conflicting, interests. But doesn't that describe all societies? And come to think of it, couldn't that also be said of most organizations?

Political organizations

So a question presents itself: are all organizations political? Think about your own company and answer the following questions:

- Are budgets tight?
- Are there more jobs at the bottom of the corporate ladder, than there are at the top?
- Do some people appear to have more "clout" than their position in the food chain merits – and more than others of identical grade?
- Are some individuals always better informed about what's going on than others?
- Do people have different interests – both corporate and personal?
- Does decision making tend to take place through informal channels?

If the answer to any of these questions – let alone all of them – is yes, then your organization *is* political. And it's a rare company that fails to score at least five out of six. So office politics is a fact of life. But is it *always* negative? Certainly, most dictionary definitions carry the pejorative and sinister connotations. Office politics is something devious and underhand. It's about advancing your own agenda at the expense of others and of the organization's goals. It's about stitching up enemies, making yourself look good, and getting the lion's share of power and glory. So does this mean that all we can look forward to at work is an unending diet of watching our backs and "dog eat dog"? *What does office politics really involve?*

According to one definition it is the covert, rather than the overt, way of getting things done. Certainly, the assumption that office politics is informal rather than formal is well accepted. So it's the stuff that the company manual doesn't tell you – activities that are outside your job description, not covered during your induction programme. But more than that, office politics implies the acquisition and utilization of power to achieve what you want to achieve. This practice can be both *constructive* and *destructive*. It can be driven by selfless concern for the general corporate good or by purely selfish motives: on the one hand public spirited, on the other, entirely self-seeking. So you need to interpret whether the individual is working the system to get a result for the organization, or for themselves.

Effective office politicians

Effective office politicians are those people who know where the power lies, understand how to obtain it for themselves, and possess the skill to use it in the pursuance of goals. This is *constructive* when the individual is concerned for the organization's or team's success, but is *destructive* when motivation is selfish or unethical, or if unacceptable methods are employed to achieve its ends. Take a look at the table below:

She is incredibly manipulative.	She is very influential.
They're such a political team.	They're just trying to get the job done.
Divide and rule is the game around here.	Internal competition is healthy.
The grapevine is rife.	I tip people off when I'm in the know.
The boss's favourites are the ones who get promotion/ the best projects etc.	The best performers are the ones who get promotion/the best projects etc.
It's not what you know, but who you know.	It's important to network with people across the business.
They're up to something.	I can't wait to hear the new direction of the company.

The left-hand column contains comments you would expect to hear in highly political organizations. An alternative view of the same situation is represented in the right-hand column. People will interpret things differently according to their position and their state of mind. Consequently, the reasons why one person will fall into one camp or the other can be diverse...

"I'm on the inside" vs "I'm on the outside"

First, are you the perceived instigator, or the victim of office politics? If you, or your team, are the instigators, you are far more likely to be generous in your account of events (right-hand column), while observers, or those on the receiving end, will tend to be more negative. The feeling of being in the A-team or the B-team, an insider or an outsider, the core or the periphery, is common in organizational life.

At a personal level, if you don't consider yourself to be a particular favourite of your boss, you may well complain that there is politics at work and consider yourself at a disadvantage, or even victimized. On a larger scale, people in branches are often very negative about the influence of – and methods employed by – head office. The power lies at the centre – well, that's the perception, even if it's not the reality – and people want a bit of it. Take the upper echelons of the British Civil Service for example. It's almost a religious conviction that you *do not* accept an appointment in a Government office outside Whitehall, even on promotion – not, that is, unless you want to give up all the power and influence you've managed to acquire over the years. This is clearly related to the old mandarin mantra that they'd rather see a £5 note torn up in the street in Whitehall, than one well-spent in Newcastle-upon-Tyne!

"Politics is a fact of life" vs "Politics is an unnecessary evil"

The second factor relates to how skilled you are in the art of office politics. It sounds obvious, but the 1998 study conducted by Nicholson McBride clearly illustrated that those managers who felt it important to understand and work the politics, were also those who held the most positive and constructive view of what it could do for an organization. Those who couldn't be bothered with politics, or even couldn't bear the thought of it, considered it to be destructive and unhelpful. This personal view will clearly have a bearing on whether the individual falls into the left or the right camp.

"This is a great place to work" vs "This place is a nightmare"

The third factor is the climate of the organization. "Political" organizations tend to be characterized by poor morale, low trust and a lack of openness. In these circumstances, people are likely to be distrustful of motives, there will be a feeling of "us and them" and rumours will be rife. But don't be misled: office politics still goes on in companies with open and trusting climates, in which people are highly motivated. It's just that the associated behaviours tend to be described more positively – as actively influencing decisions, communicating effectively and networking, for instance.

"There's not too much of it around" vs "There's a lot of it around"

The fourth and final factor is related to the scale of the problem – just how much destructive politicking goes on around here? We've established that office politics, in its broadest sense, is at work in all organizations. But it would be inaccurate to suggest that political activity is always on the same scale. Companies at the high end of the scale (and probably the ones with problems in this area) are likely to be those where some or all of the following apply:

Excessive competition at the top. This is likely to create competition lower down in the organization and may also indicate disagreement about the direction of the company. Conflicts of interest and personality are likely to be common.

Ambiguous goals. In this sort of situation, you find people redefining the goals to suit their own purposes. Managers are well placed to empire-build, and conflicts tend to arise between departments.

Complex structures. Any organizational structure that creates ambiguity or dual accountability is likely also to provoke a higher level of political activity – both constructive and destructive – purely because of the set-up. There is a risk of ambiguity, and success will require a great deal of negotiation and co-operation. It is common, therefore, to find individuals vying for power and influence.

High level of change. Office politics increases in situations where policy and procedures are not clearly laid out. When there is a high degree of change, it is often not possible – nor desirable – to keep rewriting the rule book. This triggers political behaviour as rival factions – and alternative interpretations of the smoke signals coming out of the board room – struggle for ascendancy.

Refusal by powerful people to change. When those in influential positions refuse to toe the corporate line, this can spark political battles throughout the organization. This sort of situation will be characterized by lip service, rivalry between different teams, and destructive game playing in the board room. A director in a FTSE 100 company recently described the bickering and point-scoring of his colleagues as being like watching a circus. At the end of the board meeting, he suggested that they should charge for tickets!

No clear definition of performance. Where it is unclear what you need to do to get on – or even to get a favourable appraisal – the chances of politicking will be high. It will be necessary to draw attention to yourself, to play up successes and divert failures, and to ingratiate yourself with your bosses. Clear remuneration and reward systems, along with honest and clear career planning, reduce this type of behaviour.

Punishment culture. When the organization is tough on poor performers, or likes to publicize failures as a warning to others, it becomes very important for people to cover their tracks carefully and ensure that nothing that goes wrong can be traced back to them. If the worst happens, it is essential to have convincing scapegoats waiting to be herded in. This type of culture provides fertile breeding ground for political animals.

Limited resources. When teams have to compete for headcount and budget, they will need to exert political influence in order to ensure that their work is regarded as an organizational priority.

Summary

People can use the phrase "office politics" glibly, as shorthand for dissatisfaction. They're often surprised by the level of "politicking" that goes on inside companies, but what they're describing is the inevitable effect of operating in an organizational environment – with conflicting objectives, clashing priorities, different styles and the operation of both formal and informal mechanisms.

It's important to view the situation as objectively as you possibly can, and examine *your position* and *your interpretation* of events. A field manager of a large manufacturing company, promoted to head office, just couldn't believe the degree of office politics at work – but actually, he just wasn't used to it. What he was describing was corporate reality, and what he needed to do was to learn to live in it, proactively, productively and without becoming a victim.

In summary, office politics can be defined as the informal, rather than the formal, way of getting things done. We also need to bear in mind that politicking can be constructive as well as destructive. So, when motives are pure, methods are confined within the limits of reasonable behaviour, and the company's performance is on the up, then office politics may not be too bad a thing. It's also likely that the incidence of political behaviour in the office will be kept to a minimum – because it's simply not needed. It's when the opposite of these conditions prevails that the nightmare scenario view of office politics comes into its own!

CHAPTER 2

Who are the office politicians?

> Question: "Who are the office politicians?" Answer: "Other people!"
> Question: "Why do they do it?" Answer: "Because they are insecure
> in their business and private lives." "Out of sheer malevolence."
> "Because they like to play games, with people or policies." "Because
> there is *always* a hidden agenda." "Because they are bored, with
> time on their hands." "To avoid exposing inadequacies." "Because
> it's the only way to get things done."
>
> More and more people admit that an understanding of, and an
> ability to manage, politics is important if you are to succeed in the
> business world these days, but still very few people admit to doing
> it themselves. Just who *are* the office politicians?
>
> **Taken from Office Politics Survey, Nicholson McBride, 1998**

Introduction

The pace of change has increased dramatically over recent years.
As a result, organizations now have to run to stand still. No
sooner has the last big idea been half-implemented, than it's time
to move on to the next. No chance to embed the changes; little
hope of things settling down. And this inevitably means fewer
rules, regulations and procedures – it's impossible to legislate for
everything. Company policy may not be up for grabs, but it's
certainly open to interpretation by acute operators.

This is fertile ground for office politics, and the types of conditions in which office politicians thrive.

Recent research findings are clear-cut: people who get on at work these days tend to be politically adept. They understand that all organizations are political systems. Perhaps more importantly, they know how to work them: if you want to get funding/win people over/get the credit/get on, you need to be proactive. In these circumstances, it's somewhat surprising that the term *office politics* continues to have negative connotations. More often than not, office politics is a label reserved for behaviours which are underhand, manipulative or damaging to others. *Constructive* office politicians, however, are described differently – perhaps as effective strategists, skilful influencers or even powerful leaders.

Behaviour

It stands to reason then that if you are going to survive in the corporate jungle you need to confront behaviours you don't believe to be constructive. Challenge your own motives too, because it's important to be able to distinguish between *constructive* and *destructive* politics. To do so, you need to scrutinize two key factors: *motivation* and *competence*.

As we saw in the previous chapter, an individual who is driven by entirely selfish motives and likes to play games with other people's emotions is a quite different animal from someone who has the best interests of the business at heart.

Equally, someone who is a past master at getting to happen what they want to happen needs to be distinguished from someone who – even when driven by the purest motives – can't resist the opportunity to rub others up the wrong way, and shows little interest in exerting a real influence on events. Such individuals are particularly prone to what psychologists call *super-ego-tripping*. That's when you judge the effectiveness of your own actions simply by how you end up feeling, regardless of what impact, if any, you may have had on events or other people.

The matrix opposite plots the situation visually. The "competence" axis relates to the ability of the individual to understand and play the politics of an organization. While the

Competence

		Bad	Good
Motives	**Good**	1. Naïve	2. Star
	Bad	3. Loser	4. Machiavellian

"motives" axis is more concerned with *why* they would want to. Boxes 1 and 2 contain people who are driven by altruistic motives. "Stars" possess the political skill required to operate effectively in an organizational context. They are often both competent and admired, whereas "Naïves" are well-intentioned, but don't have the political skill to achieve their objectives. They may be perceived as irritants, innocents, militants or simply well-meaning incompetents.

In boxes 3 and 4 we have people who are driven by suspect motives – politicians in the most negative sense of the word.

450 years after its publication, Niccolo Machiavelli's tract *The Prince* remains the most chilling application of the belief that the end justifies the means. Frustrated by the constant political turbulence of the times he lived in, Machiavelli's advice to governments reflected his conviction that the political status quo must be protected at any cost. "Machiavellian" therefore is the description reserved for those people, driven by "bad" motives, who are adept at understanding and interpreting situations, and making happen what they want to happen.

"Losers" are more likely to be described as politicians, since their activities are less subtle and their motives easier to read. They may be prone to misjudging situations or acting in a way that is transparently self-seeking. They certainly don't possess the political nous of the Machiavellian and are, therefore, less effective at making things happen.

Examples

Let's look at some examples in business life. Who could justify the actions of a chief executive who allows a prospective merger to founder – in the process squandering the opportunity to create billions of pounds of extra shareholder value – purely out of fear that it might weaken their own personal position? Such an individual clearly belongs in Box 3.

It is more difficult to diagnose the motivation of someone who fights tooth and nail, and invests massive amounts of money, to undermine the strategy of a key competitor – ostensibly to safeguard consumer interests, though they themselves stand to make substantial personal gain. Where do they belong?

And how about the person who indulges in politics purely because they *enjoy* it? This animal is someone who gets a kick out of playing one person off against another. They consider it a matter of personal honour to beat an internal rival – whether it's in the company's interests or not. They delight in making others squirm by exploiting difficult inter-personal dynamics. For them, a day in the office is not complete without some political fun. Bad motives again.

You may be able to spot people like that, but are they able to spot themselves? How many people have you ever heard own up to behaviour like this? It's striking how effective such individuals can be at justifying their actions. In the same way, powerful and articulate leaders are often adept at positioning manipulative and self-serving actions as being in the best interests of the company, consumers or even the community as a whole.

Are you a victim?

So the situation is not straightforward. You have to recognize that behaviour is political and then assess whether it is being done for "good" or "bad" reasons. Diagnosis is complex, but it's important to be aware of what's going on if you don't want to become a victim of a sophisticated political operator.

How exposed are you right now? Use the checklist opposite to assess whether destructive politics is at play in your workplace, putting a tick against those statements you think correctly apply.

	Tick
1. People find out what others are saying about them from third parties.	☐
2. It's almost impossible to keep anything quiet.	☐
3. People who get on are not the most deserving.	☐
4. People seem quick to point the finger when something goes wrong.	☐
5. There are lots of cliques.	☐
6. There are lots of informal meetings in rooms with closed doors.	☐
7. Colleagues talk about others behind their backs.	☐
8. People tend to be suspicious about decisions taken.	☐
9. People are suspicious of others' motives.	☐
10. Gossip is rife.	☐
11. You suspect that others take the credit for your successes.	☐
12. You are pressurized into doing favours for others.	☐
13. People seem to be grabbing as much turf as they can.	☐

The more of these statements that apply to your company, the more political the organization is. So thirteen ticks would be very unlucky indeed! The guidelines in Part Two of this book will help you adopt a proactive approach, recognize office politics at work, confront the issues this raises, and generally enhance your powers of influence. But this still leaves the central question unanswered: who *are* the politicians around here?

Are you a political animal?

"He's a political animal…" is a phrase you hear all the time. But how many times have you heard someone admit: "Of course I'm a political animal"? It's not companies that create politics, it's the people within them. So somebody must be at it – maybe even you! Try the quiz overleaf to assess your own OPR (Office Politics Rating). Be honest – if you cheat, you'll only be deceiving yourself!

To what extent do the statements represent your philosophy? Against each statement, award yourself "2" if you completely agree, "1" if you somewhat agree, and "0" if you disagree.

	Score		Score		Score		Score
1. I try to make others feel important by openly appreciating their work.		2. It's important to know where the power really lies in an organization.		3. It's sometimes necessary to use underhand methods to beat the competition.		4. No-one should get special treatment.	
5. I need to exert my influence to help the team achieve their goals.		6. I try to find some way of getting on with everybody.		7. I always try to make a good first impression.		8. If you have a strong argument, people will usually agree with you.	
9. I compromise on issues that are clearly more important to others.		10. I do favours for people so that I can rely on them to do favours in return.		11. I try to avoid getting involved with controversial or risky projects.		12. I firmly believe that "pulling strings" is wrong.	
13. I adapt my style when dealing with different types of people.		14. Total openness is not always the best approach.		15. The grapevine can be manipulated to help you achieve your goals.		16. Total openness and honesty is always the best approach.	
17. I do my best to protect others from the politics that go on around here.		18. It's important to pick the right time and place to deal with a difficult issue.		19. In organizational life, you sometimes have to lie.		20. Difficult issues should be dealt with instantly, no matter where you are.	
21. I avoid being totally open about people's faults, as it can hurt them badly.		22. I operate on the basis that it's not *what* you know, but *who* you know.		23. Divide and rule is a pretty effective management technique.		24. Networking is something other people do.	
25. People who are organiza-tionally naïve can get in the way of progress.		26. The pot is limited, so it's often necessary to fight for funding.		27. I would do my best to force out someone who just doesn't "cut the mustard".		28. The projects with the most merit will always get the necessary budget.	
29. I help people to save face if they make a mistake.		30. Effective networking is crucial in business these days.		31. Pulling strings and calling in favours helps you get on in life.		32. I really can't be bothered with playing the politics.	
Column 1 Total		Column 2 Total		Column 3 Total		Column 4 Total	

A score of 12 or more in any one column is a high score.

A high score in Column 2 suggests that you *are* a political animal, but it is important to view this in conjunction with Columns 1 and 3, which indicate your *motivation* for political behaviour.

A high score in Column 1 suggests you are interested in making progress and helping the team – a Star, perhaps. Column 3 is more to do with seeking personal gain – 12 indicates a Machiavellian/Loser on a grand scale, but beware if you have 8 or more in this column.

A high score in Column 4 indicates that you are not at all a political animal, but that you would benefit from learning some lessons in how to achieve your objectives. Again, this scale needs to be viewed in conjunction with Columns 1 and 3, which indicate your *motivation*. A high score in Column 1 suggests you are well-intentioned, perhaps more Naïve than Loser. Again, watch out for a high score in Column 3.

Plot your scores on the matrix below, remembering that zero is at the centre:

● Take your total score from Column 1 and, working up from the centre, place a cross at the appropriate point on the vertical axis.

● Starting at the centre and working right, add your total from Column 2 to the horizontal axis.

● Working down from the centre, mark your Column 3 score on the vertical axis.

● Finally, starting at the centre and working left, add your Column 4 score.

● Join the four points.

Competence

	Bad		**Good**

			16	Column 1 Total
			14	
Good			12	
			10	
	1. Naïve		8	2. Star
			6	
			4	
Motives			2	
	16 14 12 10 8 6 4 2	2 4 6 8 10 12 14 16		
	Column 4 Total		2	Column 2 Total
			4	
			6	
Bad	3. Loser		8	4. Machiavellian
			10	
			12	
			14	
			16	Column 3 Total

So what does it mean? Use the following guide to get a feel for where you fall on this diagram.

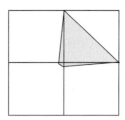

Perfect Star. There's not a lot you don't know about making things happen in the most positive way. But put it to the test, ask someone else to complete the questionnaire about you – just in case they don't share your view!

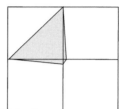

Absolute Naïve. Your heart is certainly in the right place, but there's a huge amount you could do to improve your effectiveness and get better results.

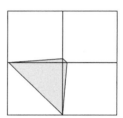

Utter Loser. You need to examine your motives for doing things – and how you operate. Do you want to stay in this box? You don't have to!

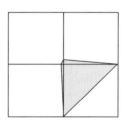

Complete Machiavellian. You firmly believe that the end justifies the means and are excellent at manipulating situations and people to get what you want. But what are you fighting for? Why not put your skills to better use and try to achieve something for the good of the whole organization?

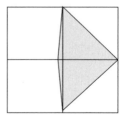

Confirmed Politician. You are effective and influential, but sometimes your motives are sound and sometimes they're not. Could it be that you're more interested in playing the game, than the result itself? Try to reduce "below the line" activity to clean up your act.

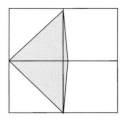

Incompetent Tinker. You like to make things happen, but somehow your actions don't seem to pay off. Try to focus your efforts "above the line" and learn how to make things happen more smoothly and effectively.

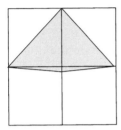

Well-Meaning Activist. You are always fighting for a cause – often unselfishly – but sometimes you go about it in a clumsy or incompetent way. Keep on fighting, but give some thought to how you can achieve a win-win situation more often.

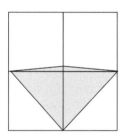

Unpredictable Snake. You are not interested in the good of the whole, nor in win-win situations. Your motives are sadly suspect. Your actions can be transparent to others, but at other times not. Examine both your methods and your motives.

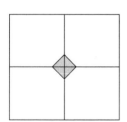

Passive Force. You don't do anyone any harm, but then you don't do much good either. You are more of a reactive than a proactive force. Think about how you could have more impact, focusing of course on moving up and right on the matrix towards the Star category.

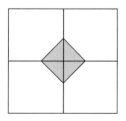

Embryonic Player. You have the potential to do more. You also have the potential to move in any direction. Analyse how you could make more of a difference in a positive way and how you could reduce any traces of incompetence or selfish motives.

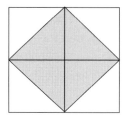

Loose Cannon. High scores on all four scales would be unusual indeed, but if you do fall into this category you need to analyse your actions carefully. In what situations do you act in a well-intentioned way? What causes you to do otherwise? Similarly, when would you be an influential force and when would you bungle it?

These graphs all illustrate extreme positions. You are unlikely to fall precisely into one category. Basically, you are looking to eliminate any behaviours that fall into the bottom half of the matrix. In addition, you should be aiming to push your scores up the "competence" scale to enhance your overall effectiveness.

To help you interpret these scores further, challenge yourself on two fronts.

Challenge 1. What *is* your motivation? *Why* are you playing the politics? Is it truly because you want the team to be successful, or is it because you want to shine personally? Is it because it's the only way to get things moving, or is it because you thrive on the game playing? Is it because you are protecting others, or is it because you doubt your own ability and their success threatens you? Question your motives. Challenge yourself. Understand why you behave as you do. There's nothing wrong with a win-win situation, but if your success means another's failure, what's the likely impact on them – and on others in the company? Every time you have a difficult decision to make, try the ethics test outlined in the diagram opposite.

Challenge 2. It's equally important to think about the *way* you do things. There is a difference between influence and manipulation, as there's a difference between constructively handling conflict and bullying. It's all in the way you do it.

Here, too, you need to examine your own approach. Be honest. Are there things you do that you're not proud of? Do you feel that you could be more effective if you modified your style in some way?

So, you do need political acumen to survive and thrive in the corporate world – without it, you are unlikely to be sufficiently

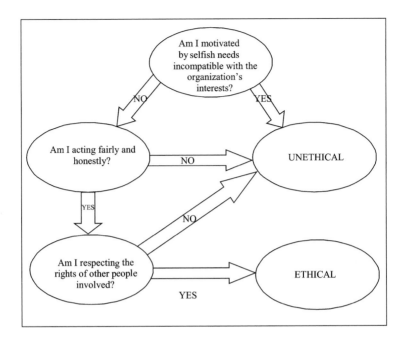

tuned in to know what to do and how to do it. But this is quite a different thing from the manipulation of events for selfish reasons, and enjoying the cut and thrust of playing one person off against another. Motives and competence are all-important in determining which camp you fall into – are you primarily Star or Loser, Machiavellian or Naïve?

Whatever your response, this book is focused on helping you become more of a Star at work.

CHAPTER 3

Adopting a positive proactive approach

"If you think you can, or you think you can't, you're probably right!"
Mark Twain

Introduction

Think about the people in your organization. How many of them truly make a difference? Or more to the point, how many of them make as *much* difference as they could do if they really put their mind to it? The answer is probably depressing. It's a fact of life that it's easier to criticize others' actions and complain about the sorry state of affairs, than it is to do something about it. Not only is it easier, but if we're honest with ourselves, it's more fun too. Gossiping and a good group moan has a sort of therapeutic effect; changing the situation is just hard work.

Then there's the "not my sort of thing" brigade – those people who state with significant conviction that they have no time for office politics. They are the ones who seem glued to their desks, who don't get out and network with other departments and then wonder why they have a hard time getting anything agreed.

Both these responses are reactive approaches. They belong to the people who don't really make a difference – or, at least, don't make the positive difference they should.

Are you reactive or proactive?

To what extent do these responses describe you? Do you complain, rather than challenge? Are you good at finding a hundred reasons why you can't do something, rather than getting on with it? Do you shy at the first hurdle, rather than finding a way to soar effortlessly over it? Or are you the sort of person who does take control and influence the situation where you can?

You can see where you stand on this by considering ten short questions. Answer yes or no to each, depending on which more accurately represents your situation or view:

1. Is there some habit, such as smoking, that you'd like to break but can't?
2. Do you feel your own personality was laid down firmly by childhood experiences, so that there is little you can do to change it?
3. Do others seem to get all the breaks?
4. Do you find it a waste of time planning ahead, because something always seems to turn up to change your plans?
5. Do you find it difficult to say "no" to people?
6. Do you find yourself procrastinating and putting things off?
7. Do you often feel you are the victim of forces outside your control?
8. Do you find that other people usually get their way?
9. Do you wait for the phone to ring and then feel rejected when it doesn't?
10. Would your friends and colleagues like you to take more responsibility for things?

Reactive people

The more affirmative answers you have given to these questions, the more likely it is that you are a *reactive* rather than a *proactive* person, i.e. you let things happen to you, rather than influencing situations and taking control. But even if your answers do place you in this category, does it really matter? The short answer is yes – probably! As well as having less impact, reactive people are more likely to feel oppressed by the flow of events; in extreme cases they are prone to free-floating anxiety (worry without a specific cause) and often feel like running away. They can even make themselves ill. The condition known as "learned helplessness" – characterized by the feeling that whatever you do, it won't make a difference – is a recognized symptom of clinical depression. Reactive people are also more likely to be victims of bullies and destructive office politicians, who are rarely inclined to pick on stronger, more assertive people. Less drastically, reactive people are often considered to be frustrating people to have around, because of their apparent lack of drive – and constant complaining.

But reactive people aren't always the shrinking violet type. There are also the people who could be described as "passive aggressives". Yes, they make their voices heard; yes, you know they're unhappy with the situation. But what they rarely focus on is actions that *they* could take to make a positive difference.

Proactive people

Genuinely proactive people do make things happen in a way that seems well-suited to the situation. These are the people we tend to admire – the winners. They're the ones who work themselves into the best jobs, are full of self-confidence, appear to be on top of things and seem able to deal with anything that life throws at them. Of course, they run the risk of being envied rather than admired by those less assured than themselves, but they are usually judged to be a positive influence and stimulating companions. So before reading on, ask yourself two further questions – answer honestly:

● Do I *really* want to change the situation?
● Do I know *how* to change the situation?

If the answer to the first question is *yes*, then Part Two of this book will help you with the second! It strongly advocates a proactive approach, whether you are dealing with a perceived injustice, or merely ensuring that your powers of influence and persuasion are up to scratch. It won't turn you into what others would describe as a political animal. Instead it's all about coping and dealing constructively with issues, making sure that you aren't a victim of destructive office politics – either of your own making, or at the hands of others.

The book is for anyone who works in a company – at whatever level and in whatever industry. It works on the basis that, in business life, you have two types of situations to deal with: exploiting opportunities and dealing with problems. With Part One looking at the background to office politics, each chapter in Part Two deals with a specific issue, so the book can either be read cover to cover, or dipped into when you have a particular need. Part Two deals with the following topics:

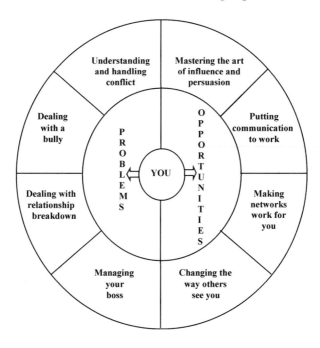

The final chapter – *The Manager's Guide To Managing Politics* – has been specifically included for anyone who happens to be in a managerial position. Clearly, managers have to deal with all the aspects of business life described in the diagram above. They also, however, have an opportunity to minimize office politics in their own team and to exert significant influence up the line in an attempt to change things on a wider basis. This chapter provides a template to help them achieve this.

Part Two

CHAPTER 4

Mastering the art of influence and persuasion

Behind the scenes lobbying to get what you want, publicly criticizing your opponent's plans, and planting your ideas in the heads of senior managers – so that they think the ideas are their own – are three activities commonly associated with office politics. This can relate to who gets which office, or which secretary. Or it can be more significant. In a large UK insurance company, Division A launched a range of new products which overlapped somewhat with those of Division B. On the face of it, the managing director of Division B offered support and co-operation, but in private he was quietly undermining the reputation and ability of Division A. The support given was always too little, too late. Ultimately the product failed, and was transferred to Division B. The managing director of Division A lost his battle to become chief executive because of his inability to administer this business.

This is a classic example of internal competition getting in the way of the overall success of the business, and of how politicking can be used to manipulate an outcome.

Introduction

In Chapter 3, we stressed the importance of taking a positive proactive approach. This is fundamental: you're unlikely to have an impact on events and achieve your aims, unless you are prepared to take action. But there are those people around us who, with the best will in the world, seem completely unable to get others to do what they want them to do. Or worse still, they manage to provoke precisely the opposite reaction. These people are ineffective influencers – irrespective of how good their ideas are objectively, other people seem determined to thwart them.

What is influence?

One definition of influence is getting others to do what you want them to do. Ideally, they do it because they want to, they see the sense, they are excited by the prospect, or whatever. More precarious is the situation where people conform to your requests, but are unhappy about it. However, this can happen – if you are dealing with an unpleasant task, for instance, or the power of your argument is so compelling that, despite reluctance, the individual has no choice but to comply.

The type of influencing style you use must be appropriate for the specific situation and the different audiences you are dealing with. More about this later! There are, however, some *general* principles that apply when you are planning to influence another person:

● Put yourself in the shoes of the recipient – what would be a good outcome for them, what are they thinking and feeling? The more you understand their motivations and concerns the more in tune with them you become, and the more likely you are to be able to influence them.

● Concentrate on the recipient – make eye contact, exchange glances and form an alliance with them.

● Demonstrate mutual understanding and common goals – if you talk about "we", rather than "I", you are instantly indicating that you are in this together. This simple switch in language can also change the emphasis from a debate which is potentially adversarial, to one which is focused on problem solving.

● Concentrate on your non-verbal signals – gestures, posture and tone of voice send far more information to the other person than the words you are using. It is therefore important to make sure that your non-verbal behaviours all add up to: "I am trustworthy and I want this to work". The easiest way to ensure that this is the case, is to be genuine:

  – go through in advance what you want to achieve and why
  – feel comfortable about what you are asking for
  – be open and honest, while remaining sensitive to the other
    person's needs, wants and feelings
  – be truly committed to a win-win situation.
● Listen!

Listening

This last point is so fundamental to being an effective influencer
that it merits a section of its own!

A director of a large retail bank expressed surprise that
listening is considered to be a part of the overall influence and
persuasion toolkit. "But surely," he said, "you're not going to be
able to persuade anyone of anything if you're just sitting there
listening." He wasn't convinced until a colleague used the analogy
of a salesperson: "Who would you prefer to buy from – the
person who bores you rigid for hours about product features etc,
or the one who listens carefully to your issues, seems to
understand them, and then comes up at the end with a solution
to your problems?" He was then convinced.

But listening is quite difficult to do properly. You need terrific
powers of concentration and tenacity to listen 100% of the time.
There are also different levels of listening:

Level 1: Listening superficially. This is where we merely pick
up the thread of what a person is saying. We may be able to repeat
the last five words they've used, but we haven't *really* heard them.
This type of conversation tends to be very one-way and the
individual doing the talking will tend to lose confidence and
interest in what they themselves are saying.

Level 2: Listening for information. Here we pick up all the
facts and figures and are listening on the surface, but we are
unaware of the feelings and emotions which accompany what the
individual is saying. The conversation will be more two-way than
at Level 1, but the type of question asked will be all about what
happened and when did it happen – questions designed to elicit
hard data. In this situation we can find ourselves ignoring pleas
for help and fixing symptoms rather than causes.

Level 3: Listening for feelings and emotions. Here we are much more aware of what is going on behind the words. We are watching for the non-verbal signals and probing far more in our questioning. The type of question asked will be about *why* things happened, or *why* an individual feels that way. This enables the listener to get to the heart of the problem. It also makes the other individual feel important and valued as a person – a very persuasive mix.

These are the basic rules. If you haven't adhered to them in the past, and you start to do so now, your ability to influence will increase. However, it's not quite as straightforward as all that! Different people like different things. What will appeal to one individual – and get them to sign on the dotted line for you – may be a real turn-off for another. You need to be able to gauge the individual, and the situation, and then apply an appropriate style. In order to be successful, the tactic you choose should be:

- ethical and socially acceptable
- used for a legitimate request
- appropriate, given your status and relationship with the person you are trying to influence
- skilfully used
- consistent with the individual's values.

Influencing techniques

Broadly speaking, influencing tactics fall into two different categories: *push* techniques, which actively steer an individual towards a particular course of action; and *pull* techniques, which are far more subtle and tend to draw the individual in. While it is artificial to draw a distinct line between the two, push actions are more akin to persuasion, and pull techniques associated with influence.

Where would you say you fall? Think about the influencing techniques that you use from day-to-day. Then answer the questions opposite, awarding yourself the appropriate score according to whether you use this type of technique:

- **Never** .... score 1 point
- **Occasionally** .... score 2 points
- **An average amount** .... score 3 points
- **Fairly frequently** .... score 4 points
- **Very frequently** .... score 5 points

	Score		Score		Score		Score
1. I appeal to others' values and aspirations.		2. I am careful to listen to others.		3. I am always ready with the facts and figures to back my argument.		4. I'm not averse to exchanging favours in order to get things done.	
5. I excite others by the way I speak.		6. I readily admit to things I have done wrong.		7. I can quickly see flaws in others' ideas.		8. I make it clear to people what I expect from them.	
9. I focus on team achievement.		10. I seek others' suggestions before offering my own ideas.		11. I can be relied on to come up with a new idea.		12. I reward people for their success.	
13. I appeal to common goals and objectives.		14. I am open about my own personal concerns.		15. I am prepared to enlist others to back my argument.		16. I'm not afraid to deal with poor performance.	
17. I can put into words things that other people only dream about.		18. I give people responsibility for important tasks.		19. I will use my position/status to get my proposals agreed.		20. I apply pressure where necessary to get what I want done.	
21. I generate a feeling of "we're in this together".		22. I really try to put myself into the shoes of others.		23. I love the cut and thrust of a good logical debate.		24. I like to bargain and negotiate with people.	
25. I am confident that we can achieve.		26. I always make sure that I have understood properly.		27. I am usually ready with a counter argument.		28. I believe that most people are motivated by fear or greed.	
29. I am able to paint a very vivid and exciting picture.		30. I make sure that everyone has a chance to voice their opinion.		31. I am happy to defend my ideas.		32. I always praise people for a job well done.	
Column 1 Total		**Column 2 Total**		**Column 3 Total**		**Column 4 Total**	

The higher you score in any one column, the more likely you are to use a particular influencing technique (described below). A score of 28 or more in any one column is a high score. It means that you range between using the influencing styles and techniques described an average amount to a frequent amount. However, this is not just about high or low scores – one person could award themselves all 5s, while someone else, who behaves in a similar way, awards 3s and 4s. Instead, it is thinking about the appropriateness of the techniques you are using: is your approach right, given the circumstances and the individual concerned?

Study the paragraphs below, which outline the techniques described in each column.

Column 1: The inspirational

This is a pull technique. It is all about painting an exciting vision – whether that's the direction of the company, or organizing the Christmas party – and generating a sense of excitement in others. People will positively want to be a part of your department/ project team/gang! It's also about focusing people on the needs of the team, by appealing to their values and aspirations.

It is most appropriate for people who are in a team leadership role and, on the whole, people who are described as inspirational and motivational will be adept at using this particular influencing style.

Column 2: The personal

This too is a pull technique. It really focuses on the individual. Being influenced in this way tends to make people feel valued and valuable, because they have been listened to, their ideas have been understood and the other person has opened up to them. It creates loyalty and trust in a team, and a spirit of selflessness and sacrifice. This influencing technique can be used in all directions – with your boss, your team and your peers – and it increases commitment to tasks.

Column 3: The logical

This is a push technique. It involves doing your homework, having all the facts and figures at your fingertips, and being prepared to argue your corner – no matter how heated the debate becomes. This is a rational rather than an emotional style of influence. It is appropriate in situations where it is important to have a watertight case: for example, when you are asking management to invest in a project. In this instance, it's vital to assess the costs, articulate the benefits and be able to back your argument cogently. The slight down-side is that people know they are being persuaded and can feel resentful. Used appropriately, however, the logical technique can be used to influence in any direction, but is *particularly* effective with your boss, or with colleagues in other departments over whom you have no direct authority. The reason for this is that the arguments are often so compelling that the risks seem minimized, the rewards tangible and the whole business case clear. It is also useful to bear in mind when you are dealing with very logical and/or risk averse people – almost irrespective of their position in the organization and the subject matter.

Column 4: The forceful

Again, this is a push technique – the carrot and stick were made for this individual! The technique involves stating clearly what is expected from people, rewarding them for success and, of course, punishing them for failures. Achieving goals is very important and so the individual will not be averse to calling in favours or applying pressure – anything to get the job done. This technique does not work well with anyone outside the team over which you have direct control. And being a push style, it can feel pretty uncomfortable on the receiving end. However, a low score in this column could mean that you are not being clear about what constitutes good performance. It could also mean that you are not giving your team the feedback they need – both good and bad. So before congratulating yourself on not using this form of influence, think about the impact that might have.

This may seem clear cut, but the real world is rarely so well-organized! So, in reality, you may need to use a blend of different styles to achieve your aims. The thing to remember is that the whole art of influencing is about getting inside the head of the other individual, really listening to what they are saying – and not saying – and adapting your style to help you achieve what you need to.

CHAPTER 5

Understanding and handling conflict

Dealing with conflict – or the failure to do so – is an arena rich with political potential. We asked for examples of office politics and came up with a wealth of material under this heading. The scenarios ranged from the very direct approach of calling someone to task about their actions, or asking provocative questions at a meeting – purely to embarrass/expose them in front of influential colleagues – right through to the indirect method of sending a blanket e-mail to a whole department, rather than tackling the one "culprit". The most extreme example was one company where the whole organizational structure was designed to ensure that one individual did not have to come into contact with another during the normal course of business. All this, rather than talk to the person about their shortcomings! An inability to handle conflict directly, honestly and fairly, seems a sure-fire way of getting yourself branded a political animal.

Introduction

People play games at work. Sometimes they do it deliberately. Often they are unaware of what they are doing, the impact they are having and how others are interpreting their actions. But you won't know for sure whether their acts are malicious, negligent or merely incompetent, unless you engage them in frank discussion. You must be prepared for the possibility that this will develop into a conflict situation: indeed, sometimes you'll have to insist on it, by refusing to accept evasive or incomplete explanations and politely reminding them of your rights as a colleague. Such a policy carries risks. However, nine times out of ten, effective conflict handling leads to a situation of greater understanding and more productive working relationships.

This chapter provides a framework to help you develop more constructive approaches to conflict, based around the following:

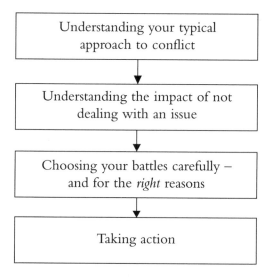

Understanding your typical approach to conflict

Cast your mind back to the last time you were angry with someone about the way they behaved, or an occasion when you were placed in an impossible situation because of another's carelessness. What were your first thoughts? Did they fall into any/all of the following categories?

Type one reaction: Oh no, hopefully things will sort themselves out!

Type two reaction: I'll deal with this next week.

Type three reaction: I'm going to give that bastard a piece of my mind – now.

Type four reaction: Let's sort this out.

Avoidance strategy

Type one reactions are an **avoidance strategy:** "If I close my eyes, and pretend nothing's happened, it may just go away." Of course it rarely does go away. All that happens is that problems fester, people continue to demonstrate unproductive behaviours and, in most cases, situations deteriorate.

Delaying strategy

Type two reactions are a **delaying strategy:** "I'm quite aware there's an issue, but I don't have the time/the nerve/the inclination to deal with it now. I'll review the situation again in a week's time and see if it's still a problem – it could well have petered out by then!"

What typically happens in this scenario is that the person keeps postponing the confrontation until such a time as it becomes just too embarrassing to deal with – the moment has passed. In other words, the type two delaying reaction has effectively become a type one avoidance reaction. You hear all the time of people who get a nasty surprise at their annual appraisal. This is often the result of these delay tactics. And their reaction? – "I really wish someone had mentioned this before."

Aggressive strategy

Type three reactions constitute an **aggressive strategy:** "How could they do this to me? By the time I've finished with them, they won't be doing it again to anyone." People who follow this behaviour pattern tend to take things very personally and don't take kindly to not getting their own way. They do not avoid issues and they do not allow problems to fester for a long time. But, while they are keen to confront problems, they tend to do it in an antagonistic ("I win, you lose") way. Very often this approach rubs people up the wrong way. It is counter-productive because human beings (unlike most other members of the animal kingdom) are programmed to respond to aggression with counter aggression, rather than submission.

Problem-solving strategy

Type four reactions involve a **problem-solving strategy:** "I don't like what's happening here, but I'm sure they had their reasons. I need to understand them. Let's learn for the future." This approach acknowledges that people act for a reason and works on the basis that, until you know what these reasons are, it's unlikely that you will be able to put in place any concrete actions for the future.

An individual using a problem-solving strategy neither avoids nor delays – nor do they charge in like a bull in a china shop. Theirs is a more co-operative, listening type of approach, which works well – except with that small, but very noticeable, sub-group who have no interest in establishing harmonious relationships. Such people – sometimes described as sociopaths – think that peaceful co-existence is for wimps, and consider a day wasted unless they have reduced a fellow human being to tears!

Which of the above approaches most closely represents your own? It may be that you react to different situations in different ways. Why? There are all sorts of reasons why we act the way we do. Below is a list of a few beliefs which can help determine why you might fail to deal with conflict effectively.

● I have no right.	● It's no big deal.
● I don't have the status.	● I can't be bothered.
● I'm not sure of my ground.	● I don't have the time.
● They intimidate me.	● They don't have the time.
● I don't like them.	● I don't *really* want to solve the problem.
● I like them.	● I don't like hurting people.
● They may stop liking me.	● It's trivial for them (but
● They may stop respecting me.	important for me).
● I'll show them who's boss.	● It's too difficult.
● I'll teach them to mess	● It's too sensitive.
with me.	● I don't have all the facts.
● I'd better get this over	● They won't change.
and done with.	

Which ones can you hear yourself saying or thinking regularly? Are there others? Think carefully and try to develop a clear picture of how you behave in different situations and with different people, and what pattern you typically fall into.

It is important to understand what motivates you – and to be prepared to challenge aspects of your own motivation. If you are really honest with yourself, you may have to admit that many of your reasons for avoiding or delaying confrontation are actually invalid. You have the right to tackle another human being about issues of mutual concern. If you find it uncomfortable to exercise this right, it's a problem worth addressing. You'll need to start by identifying causes: is it low self-esteem, or perhaps the fear of failure that is holding you back? Maybe you don't really want to solve the problem – you're happier to sit back and moan about it, playing the martyr. Or it could be that you just want to give the other person a piece of your mind.

Successful conflict resolution requires two things. The first is a *real* desire to solve the problem. The second is the ability to view the situation objectively – even if it is a very personal issue – and develop an approach that is focused on solving the problem, not merely making yourself feel better.

Understanding the impact of not dealing with an issue

Why is it so harmful to avoid dealing with an issue? Surely it's better to keep quiet, maintain the stiff upper lip, than it is to risk hurting another's feelings and damaging the relationship. Not so! There are three potential down-sides to suppressing conflict and keeping a lid on things:

Damage to you. Bottling things up and worrying constantly about what people are thinking and saying about you are significant stressors. They can seriously damage your wellbeing – and your health. So you owe it to yourself to get issues out into the open and solve them.

Damage to others. This applies both to the individual, or individuals, involved in the conflict, and to innocent bystanders. The impact of workplace tensions can cause serious ripples – sometimes throughout the organization.

Damage to the organization. Inter-personal conflicts of whatever nature will inevitably impact on the organization. Time wasted gossiping or backstabbing damages the company's interest. But frequently, conflicts are not actually personal, they are organizational. You feel that others are not maintaining standards, or living the company values. Refusing to air these issues results in continued clashes over approach. The quality of work suffers, and customers may receive inconsistent and shoddy service.

And how will other people react to the confrontational approach? They may be surprisingly willing to hear feedback – not everyone conforms to Noel Coward's observation: "I can take any amount of criticism, so long as it is unqualified praise!" If the news is bad, people may not seem grateful at the time to hear it. They may react aggressively. But in the long run, most people think it's better to know, than to be kept in the dark about things they are doing that others would rather they did differently – or not at all.

This applies up to – and especially at – the top of an organization. Most senior managers consider "the top" to be a lonely place indeed. They do not get enough feedback because the people who report to them are too scared, or too obsequious, to tell them where they're going wrong. Instead, they tell them what they think they want to hear. As a consequence, senior managers can go about their business, completely unaware that their style is inappropriate, or that they are seen as bullies, underminers, destroyers, sycophants, etc.

Choosing your battles carefully – and for the *right* reasons

One word of warning before moving on to how to handle conflict effectively: you don't have to fight a battle every time the opportunity arises. Irrespective of your personal feelings, there is only one question you need to ask yourself in determining whether or not to challenge an individual about a particular issue: what will the impact be if this issue is *not* addressed?

- Will another person continue to perform in a sub-standard way – no matter how slight the defect is?
- Will the organization suffer in any way – internally or externally?
- Will you continue to brood about the other person's actions?
- Will others feel bad?

If the answer to any of these questions is yes, then you may well need to act. If not, you will probably be best advised to keep your powder dry for the next flashpoint that *really* matters!

Taking action

We have examined your typical approach to conflict and developed a clear picture of how you behave in certain situations. We have also explored the implications of not tackling an issue. So what happens when you decide to move towards confrontation − i.e. to *act*?

How do you maximize your chances of successfully clearing the air, and minimize the risk of making things worse? The first thing to do is to think about how you typically behave when you have to give someone feedback. This will help you to anticipate things which are likely to go wrong. Look at the statements below and place a tick in the box if you think they correctly apply to you.

1.	Tick
Your criticism of other people is often destructive	☐
People don't seem to recognize the value of your praise	☐
You tend to ignore strengths and seize upon weaknesses	☐
You are constantly finding fault	☐
You are a perfectionist − nothing is ever good enough	☐
You are almost entirely task-driven	☐
You don't see the harm in giving negative feedback through impersonal channels such as e-mail	☐

2.	Tick
You often refer to previous mistakes	☐
You are not worried about putting people down in public	☐
You sometimes look for scapegoats	☐
You sometimes take the credit for other people's improvements/achievements	☐
Positive feedback is not your "thing"	☐
You fear that your methods are driven by personal insecurities	☐
You feel threatened by other people	☐

3.	Tick
You sometimes pay lip service to things	☐
You give too many easy, positive "strokes"	☐
You give feedback mechanically, without seeing its real worth	☐
You shy away from giving bad news and honest assessments	☐
You often avoid the real issue, and go off the point	☐
You want to be liked by everyone	☐
Your assessments are vague and general	☐

Each of the three sections represents a different style of feedback – all negative. Add up the number of ticks you scored in each section and write your score against 1, 2 and 3 in the table below.

Negative feedback style	Total ticked	Subliminal message to others
1. The Destroyer		'Fear me'
2. The Underminer		'Respect me'
3. The Easy Timer		'Love me'

The Destroyer. If you have ticked a number of boxes in this first section, you run the risk of being the type of person who is always quick to find fault in others' work, but rarely, if ever, gives any praise. You act quickly. You are direct, but sometimes quite damaging in your feedback.

The impact of this can be that others are fearful of making mistakes and being found out. They therefore play safe and rarely enter into honest discussions with you. You may suffer, because people are resistant to your message before you even start and your words fall on deaf ears.

The Underminer. A number of ticks in the second section indicates a more undermining style. Rather than give bad news directly like the destroyer, you have a more subtle approach. You may be king of the back-handed compliment, for instance. You want others to recognize that they owe you a lot for their successes (though their failures, of course, are always down to them!). It may be that you pursue this type of feedback style because you are insecure in your own abilities, and perhaps lack confidence. The risk here is that others feel humiliated and small. They are aware of their faults, but they don't really have much idea about how to put them right – and daren't ask you for specific advice.

The Easy Timer. A number of ticks in the third section and you are the type of person who shies away from giving negative feedback. Instead, you shower people with compliments – whether they deserve them, or not. When bad news is due, you may attribute it to other people: "Of course, *I* don't think it's an issue, but so-and-so does." The impact of this type of approach is that people do not learn. They also tend to become distrustful of your motives and may come to see you as two-faced and fickle.

This exercise will have made you examine to what extent one of three common but disfunctional feedback styles might be affecting your own effectiveness with people. There is no high, medium or low score in this exercise. Each and every tick represents something you do – or have done in the past – which is likely to get in the way of your message being received constructively. Re-examine the statements you have ticked. When do you do it? Why do you think you do it? How easy would it be for you to modify your approach?

So much for how *not* to give feedback. But how *should* it be done? Below are some tips to bear in mind when you have bad news to give:

- Be really *specific* about what exactly it is you think the person should be doing differently. Otherwise there's a real danger that your observations will be heard as "I don't like you as a person", rather than "I think you should have done this differently".
- Make sure the place is appropriate. Never criticize people in public – it is humiliating for them – choose a private room away from the rest of the team where you can both talk openly about the issue.
- Where possible, don't delay. While you occasionally need to give yourself a few minutes – or hours – to calm down, you shouldn't put off the moment for too long. It is not helpful to haul someone over the coals for an incident that happened six months ago. Nor is it best practice to allow destructive behaviour to continue for years without talking to the individual about it.
- Put the effort in – give it the importance it deserves and prepare properly. Even ten minutes' preparation – of the message you want to give, the impact you want to have and the way in which you should tackle the issue – can make all the difference to an encounter.

- Anticipate the response – how can you make the message more palatable, without undermining its impact?
- Balance positive and negative feedback.
- Deliver negative feedback in a non-critical way. If possible, de-personalize the issue: talk about a specific piece of work, rather than make blanket statements about the individual. Set it in context – particularly flagging up where the destructive behaviour or poor performance seemed out of character. Be sensitive.
- Concentrate on pitch and tone so valuable information is not seen as a complaint, criticism, moan or nag.
- Beware of being patronizing.
- Remember throughout that you want to solve the problem.

Helping someone solve a problem is very closely aligned with the art of influence and persuasion – you need to adopt a different approach with different people. It may be useful, therefore, to refer back to the previous chapter as a part of your preparation. This will help you to be clear about the type of person you are dealing with and the nature of the situation.

CHAPTER 6

Dealing with a bully

There was once a pathologist, who was widely regarded as a bully. This man wouldn't let himself be examined by others, so certain was he that he knew best. Others suspected that his diagnosis was wrong, but didn't have the nerve – or the desire – to confront him about it. Feedback and debate he considered a waste of time. And the outcome? He died – and the post-mortem revealed that the self-diagnosed "cancer" had been a perforated ulcer. The moral of this story is clear...

Introduction

Throughout this book, we have been working on the basis that office politics is the informal rather than the formal way of doing things, and that we are most concerned about such behaviour when the individual's motives are suspect and their methods are damaging. Given this definition, the bully must be the most extreme form of office politician around.

Bullies rarely confront issues in a constructive way. Nor are they prepared to compromise. Instead they employ a wide range of unacceptable techniques to undermine and – in extreme cases – wipe out the chosen target. These range from smear campaigns and "dirty tricks" at one end of the scale, to unremitting criticism and a complete failure to listen at the other. Whatever the cause, however, the impact is significant. And as more and more information comes to light on the subject, it is starting to emerge as a serious problem for organizations.

In the last chapter we dealt with how you can most effectively tackle people on issues that are concerning you. This chapter is entirely dedicated to dealing with the bully.

What is bullying?

Being bullied at work is traumatic in the extreme. And it's far more common than most people recognize. But many victims don't realize that they are being bullied, or alternatively find it difficult to admit – either to themselves, or to others.

So what is bullying? There is no standard definition, but according to Angela Ishmael in her book *Harassment, Bullying and Violence at Work*, it can be regarded as "persistent, offensive, abusive, intimidating, malicious or insulting behaviour, which amounts to an abuse of power and makes the recipient feel upset, threatened, humiliated or vulnerable. Bullying undermines the target's self-confidence and may cause them to suffer stress."

The range of negative behaviours which fit this "definition" is broad. According to Tim Field, who runs the National Workplace Advice Line (NWBAL) in the UK, bullying can include:

- Nit-picking.
- Fault-finding.
- Undermining.
- Isolation.
- Exclusion.
- Hypocrisy.
- Duplicity.
- Fabrication.
- Distortion/twisting the facts.
- Constant criticism.
- Abuse of disciplinary procedures.
- Imposition of verbal or written warnings for trivial reasons.
- Being singled out.
- Being marginalized.
- Being belittled.
- Being humiliated.
- Being shouted at.
- Being threatened.
- Being overloaded.
- Having responsibility increased but authority taken away.
- Having leave refused.
- Having training denied.
- Having unrealistic goals and deadlines imposed.

- Unfair dismissal.

- Never getting the credit for work carried out.

The perpetrators can be what Field terms "serial bullies": it's not necessarily about you – if you weren't there they'd be doing it to someone else. Indeed, they could well be giving others the same sort of treatment that they're dishing out to you. Left unchecked, this behaviour will continue. The tell-tale signs of a serial bully are as given below. He or she:

- Is a compulsive liar.
- Has a selective memory.
- Denies everything.
- Is devious, manipulative and spiteful.
- Doesn't listen.
- Can't sustain mature adult conversation.
- Lacks a conscience.
- Shows no remorse.

- Is drawn to power.
- Is ungrateful.
- Is disruptive and divisive.
- Is inflexible and selfish.
- Is insensitive.
- Is insincere.
- Is insecure and immature.
- But can also be charming and plausible.

This last point is significant. In our consultancy work, the individuals dubbed "bullies" – usually by the people who work for them – are often perceived by others as charismatic, successful and good to be with. It is often this ability to charm that allows the bully to get away with their behaviour for so long. And it's also that trait which can give them a big following amongst those who aren't being subjected to the bullying treatment.

Bullying patterns

The bullying can follow a pattern, which involves two distinct phases. The first is control and subjugation – the period during which the bully is using some or all of the above behaviours to reduce the victim's self-esteem, self-worth and self-confidence. The second is elimination – removal of the victim from the team or company. Typically, there will then be an interval and then the behaviour will start up again with a different victim.

Impact of bullying

The impact of bullying can be significant. Andrea Adams, in her book *Bullying at Work* states that one of the clearest indicators is the state of the victim's health. It is not uncommon for people to feel sick, suffer from disturbed sleep patterns, palpitations and a loss of energy, experience stomach and bowel problems or endure other minor aches and pains. Emotional symptoms are also common – anxiety, irritability, panic attacks, depression, anger and a loss of confidence can all be the result of bullying. And at the most extreme end of the scale you have wrecked lives – even suicide. When life and death matters like these are in question, it's important to act – either to deal with the bully outright, or if that's not possible, to initiate palliative measures to minimize suffering – both yours, and other people's.

Dealing with a bully

So who are the bullies, who are their victims, and what can you do if you think you're one of them?

Trades Union Congress (TUC) research suggests that in the UK five million of the current workforce have experienced bullying at work.

On 28 November 1996, the Institute of Personnel and Development (IPD) published the results of a survey revealing that one in eight (around three million) UK employees had been bullied at work in the previous five years. And a survey conducted two years earlier by Staffordshire University Business School produced even more startling results. They found that 53% (around 14 million) of UK employees had been bullied at work during their working life. And many of those responding to the surveys thought that the problem was getting worse, not better.

People in managerial and professional roles are more likely to have suffered from bullying than other types of employee. Moreover, although bullying is often thought to be something that bosses inflict on their staff, in reality it features in many different types of power relationships at work.

So what can you do if you experience bullying?

The first step is to **acknowledge the problem** to yourself. Recognize that you are being bullied, but remember that you are not alone.

It's important to resist any temptation to feel shame, embarrassment and guilt. These are normal reactions, but misplaced and inappropriate. They are the sorts of feelings that actually help abusers to control and silence their victims. Remember that many people are victims of bullying purely *because* they are good at their job and popular with people. They may have skills and attributes that the bully envies, feels desperately insecure about, and is determined to undermine.

The second step is to **inform yourself.** Read up on the subject. Visit Tim Field's website: *http://www.successunlimited.co.uk* (between 30 and 50 people visit this site every day). This is a mine of information, which is regularly updated. It points you in the direction of helplines, organizations that may be able to help, and useful reading. If you don't have access to the Internet, then ask for an information pack (phone 01235 834548, fax 01235 861721). Alternatively, contact the Andrea Adams Trust on 01273 704900.

The third step is to **take action.** It may be sufficient to confront the individual assertively, pointing out what they are doing and the impact it is having. In a number of cases the individual accused will be horrified and concerned at the way they are perceived, and may feel moved to take immediate action to address the situation. However, this is unlikely to work if the person you are dealing with is, indeed, a serious serial bully. In these cases, you would definitely be advised to seek help.

Take action
Keep information
You will need information to support your case. It is important to keep a diary of any instances of abuse or mistreatment, and take copies of relevant e-mails or memos. Remember, a one-off incident is rarely considered to constitute bullying, it is the barrage of snide and sarcastic remarks, the constant drip-feeding of unfounded allegations and the ongoing undermining of your authority and confidence. You must make sure that you have captured the *series* of events if your case is to hold water.

Equally, if you have been accused or criticized unfairly, put in writing a request for the bully to expand upon the allegation. It needs to be phrased carefully and as unemotionally as possible. Ask a trusted friend or colleague to look through it for you with a critical eye, testing for anything that could be perceived to be provocative or inflammatory. If the bully doesn't reply to your initial request, put it in writing again, commenting that you haven't received a response to your initial communication.

Seek support

So you have put together your case, but whom can you turn to? Ideally you would approach your line manager to explain what has been going on and the impact it has had – both on you and on the team. Bear in mind, however, that the bully could well *be* your line manager. If you have already tried to challenge him or her, and the situation does not improve, you will need to try a different tack. Consider the following:

- If your physical or psychological health has suffered, contact your doctor or your occupational health unit at work.
- Many unions are aware of the existence and impact of bullying at work – and are sympathetic to it. You may, therefore, be advised to talk to your union or employee representative.
- Consult your Personnel or HR department for advice.
- Contact one or more of the many helplines that have been set up to deal with just this issue – for instance, the NWBAL or the Andrea Adams Trust (see earlier for contact numbers).
- Most organizations these days have policies and guidelines to deal with such problems. Ask for a copy of your employer's bullying and harassment policy. You might wish to do this discreetly (e.g. through a third party) if you're not yet ready to challenge the bully.
- Find out about the official grievance procedure and follow it.
- Contact a lawyer.

Look after yourself

It has to be acknowledged, however, that if you have been subjected to bullying, you may not feel strong enough, brave enough, or – somewhat surprisingly – embittered enough, to take what may be considered to be drastic action like this. So how, in this situation, can you look after yourself?

The first thing to do is to examine any victim-like words, phrases and behaviours that you use. What do you do or say that might make you fair game for the office bully? Do you find yourself using any of these phrases?

- "Mustn't complain".
- "I'm sure he/she doesn't mean any harm really".
- "He/she's no doubt got his/her own problems".
- "What else can you expect?"
- "It's probably my own fault".
- "I suppose I ought to…"
- "I don't like to make waves".

Apologizing too much – even when it's clearly not your fault – always assuming the blame, and being too tolerant are all traits which will make you a fitting victim. You could also lack assertiveness (although you may behave aggressively) and you may worry too much about what others think of you. This last point is significant. Since most bullies can be very popular with others, it can be incredibly difficult to stand up to them, or take action to redress the situation.

Just like acknowledging that you are being bullied, recognizing that you may be doing things to make the situation worse is also a significant step. Make a real effort to abolish any phrases which suggest you'll always take the blame and you'll put up with anything. Become more assertive in your approach (there are many good training courses and books aimed at helping you develop in this area). Appreciate that you don't have to put up with what you have been putting up with, and play your part in stamping out this unacceptable facet of business life.

CHAPTER 7

Dealing with relationship breakdown

A director of a major project in North America suffered a complete breakdown in relationships with the rest of her project team. The situation gradually became unworkable. She communicated only by e-mail, copying negative feedback for individuals both to the rest of the team, and to the company's head office. She did not confront issues relating to individuals. Instead she discussed their shortcomings behind their backs. She lost track of what was going on with the project. The rest of the team was strong, united against a common enemy – their boss! They communicated: three times a week they went out drinking to discuss the latest misdeeds of the "boss from hell".

And why did this happen? Well, clearly things deteriorated over time, but in the first instance, there were two major causes: a lack of trust in individuals to do their jobs, and an inability to confront people directly.

Why do you want good working relationships?

Some people believe that good working relationships are nice to have – an optional extra, but not essential to the success of the business. They're wrong. Evidence suggests that a work environment where people positively respect, rather than merely tolerate, each other makes them not just happier and more satisfied at work, but also more productive and committed.

It starts at the top. Directors who get on with each other send a reassuring message to the troops: the business is in safe hands and headed in a single, agreed direction. Further down, managers who take the trouble to foster excellent relations with their teams know that they can count on them to go the extra mile when the pressure is really on.

People who actively cooperate with their counterparts in other departments are helping the company to deliver excellent service to customers, in an efficient and effective way.

But the whole notion of effective working relationships is often misunderstood, both in terms of what they are and how to develop them. This chapter aims to demystify the art of relationship building and outline what to do when they go wrong.

What is a good working relationship?

Contrary to popular belief, it's not about going out socially, being forever in one another's pockets and knowing the intimate details of other people's personal lives. It is about respect, trust, listening and empathy. It's about achieving a win–win situation, instead of one person profiting from the other's failure. And it's about working together to get the most from combined strengths. This can be difficult. The most potentially powerful relationships are those forged between individuals who are quite different from one another – they can complement one another's strengths, compensate for each other's weaknesses, and bring such completely different perspectives to bear on a situation that the result is inevitably richer and better thought through. However, these people are liable to rub each other up the wrong way.

Forging effective relationships requires you to get beyond the irritation factor, and really make something of the potential. Recognizing that someone has an alternative approach from your own is a starting point. But it's not enough. You need to be able to value their style, and reach a position where you can exploit your *collective* strengths to achieve organizational goals. For instance, a thorough, methodical worker may be intolerable to a fast-moving, target-driven type. However, the former's strengths could be put to good use in averting disaster caused by an ill-thought through strategy.

Respect

Mutual respect is a fundamental aspect of effective working relationships and a lot of research has been conducted into what creates it. The answer is unsurprising: if you genuinely respect others, they will respect you. By putting this simple principle into practice, many people have transformed both the way they feel about others, and the way they feel about themselves, just by making a concerted effort to respect others' skills.

But how do you develop respect for an individual? First, it is important to be clear about what value they add. Make a list of what they do well. Evaluate the benefits of these strengths. Consider whether the negatives could be the inevitable down-side of the positives – remember, we all have weaknesses! Try to get inside their heads and understand their motivation. Engage them in a dialogue and really listen. Give them the benefit of the doubt.

And what if you've done all this and you still can't respect the individual? It's perhaps a controversial view, but you are only entitled to adopt this position where you suspect the other person to be unethical. And if this is not the case, you have one of two paths available to you: either find something to admire in them as described above; or take the trouble to give them feedback about their performance or behaviour. Prepare your case carefully, be clear about what you want to achieve (it's not enough to dump the information on the individual, you must have a positive outcome in mind) and prepare to listen to their point of view.

Trust

Another important cornerstone of effective relationships is trust: it is vital that you have trust in others, and they have trust in you. Without this, people become suspicious, nervous, demotivated and sometimes slightly paranoid. They can spend a lot of time checking things out and covering their tracks.

And how do you develop it? Well, trust breeds trust. In other words, if you do trust others, the chances are they will trust you. But you also need to be consistent, both in terms of how you deal with people and in "walking the talk". If you say something is important, you must act accordingly, otherwise people will accuse you of paying lip service. Finally, you need to deliver what you promise. If you do all this, you will show yourself to be trustworthy.

Listening

Listening was covered in depth in Chapter 4. It is also one of the fundamentals of developing effective relationships: how can you hope to foster a relationship with someone if you don't know what they think or feel about things?

Listen carefully and patiently. Listen for feelings and emotions, as well as for facts and information. Demonstrate you've listened by playing their words back to them – not parrot-fashion, but by summarizing and checking your understanding. Many people *are* listening, but don't appear to be because they miss out this vital element of the listening process. And respond to what the other person is saying. That doesn't mean you always have to agree with them, but it does mean sharing your own feelings and thoughts on an issue.

Empathy

Empathy is the art of putting yourself in the shoes of another and understanding the way they may feel about things. It's about seeing their perspective and being on their side. And it's about striking up rapport.

You may feel that you can't possibly empathize unless you yourself have gone through a similar experience. But that's not the case. You just need to be able to use your imagination, without making what could be false assumptions. How do you do this? Well, careful questioning is one important aspect – asking the other person what they think about a situation, and what the solution might be, rather than imposing your own views. And, of course, the ability to listen to the response is fundamental here as well.

Paying close attention to body language, pace and mood is also key. Jollying someone along and trying to share your own enthusiasm will do little to shift the mood of someone who is feeling really down. Matching their style and pace, without mimicking the individual, will help far more. If appropriate, you can then start to raise your energy levels and inject some positivity – but it's critical to do this very gradually.

So that's effective working relationships – sometimes difficult to build, but certainly worthwhile once you've done it. You may also be personal friends with the individual. But that's certainly not essential, and there's no reason on earth why you can't have a perfectly adequate working relationship with someone you don't consider to be a "friend".

What happens when relationships break down?

Just as good relationships contribute to the welfare of an organization, relationship breakdowns usually cause problems.

Take an extreme example. If you have a chairman and a chief executive who can't bear to be in the same room as each other, what chance do you have of developing an effective corporate strategy? It's virtually impossible to keep a lid on this sort of situation. Employees, customers and other stakeholders will soon be talking about it, and it won't be long before the analysts and journalists pick up the story. As a result, confidence in the organization plummets.

Less dramatic, but equally damaging, are rifts between managers of departments or team leaders. Lack of co-operation, back-biting and blame are all symptoms. A "lose-lose" situation can quickly emerge: "I know that my team has failed, but it was only because those bastards in Personnel/Marketing/Sales didn't deliver – as usual." Others get sucked in and a huge amount of energy is wasted in gossiping, complaining, finger-pointing – in fact, doing everything except resolving the situation.

The complete breakdown of any relationship between two people – no matter their position in the company – will have a negative impact on the business. However, the corporate impact can pale into insignificance compared with the personal impact. At the lower end of the damage scale you find people looking for other jobs. As you move up the scale you find stress, illness – and worse. No-one wants to have enemies. No-one wants to agonize for hours about how to avoid coming into contact with someone. No-one wants to feel paranoid about what another person could be saying about them. So the problem of relationship breakdown must be addressed.

What causes breakdowns?

Like many people-related issues, diagnosis of the cause and formulation of a solution is not straightforward. There can be all sorts of reasons why people don't get on. For example:

- *Chemistry* – "I don't like you".
- *Personality/Style* – "I don't like the way you do things".
- *Philosophy/Values* – "I don't like what you stand for".
- *Conflict of interest* – "I don't like what you do, because your gain is my loss".
- *Injury* – "I don't like what you did".
- *Prejudice* – "I don't like your type of person".
- *Jealousy* – "I don't like you for what you've got".

How to deal with breakdowns

As there are a number of different *causes* of relationship breakdown, there are also a number of different types of *solution*.

Outlined below are some strategies which you can use to help mend broken relationships. Under each category are two sets of guidelines: the first is appropriate if you *personally* are involved in the breakdown; the second is designed for dealing with situations in which *other people* are involved. This is particularly relevant for those in a managerial position.

1. Chemistry
When it's you...
Chemistry is possibly one of the most difficult problems to deal with as it's not based on rational thought. The chances are you didn't like this person the moment you clapped eyes on them.

So how are you going to change that? First, challenge your assumption that the problem is chemistry alone. Has something happened which has created resentment on your part? Or is it the way they approach a task which drives you crazy? If you can't identify a specific cause, the chances are it *is* just chemistry.

Question: do they also think there's a problem? If so, you will need to speak to them. Conflict is never easy – and it's anathema to some people – but it can be made slightly more palatable if tackled in a constructive way. Think through what they're like and plan to tackle the conversation in a way that is more likely to appeal to them. Be open about the problem and seek their view. Just having the conversation could help.

If you don't think the other person is aware of the problem, then you don't necessarily need to have the discussion. Instead, convince yourself that you *can* get on with the individual. Find something to value about them, be determined to try to like them, and then treat them with the respect they deserve as a human being. Of course, it is far easier said than done, but if you succeed, you'll not only feel better about the relationship, but also about yourself.

When it's others…
If this is a problem you need to sort out in others, it's important for them to realize the damage they're causing – quickly!

Tackle each individual separately first. Give them the feedback, outline the impact and explore the reasons for their behaviour. If the problem continues, it may be necessary to talk to them together, in private. Use mediation skills to try to bring the two together, and once you've started to get movement, it may be desirable to set them a joint task. You need to be convinced that they want to make it work, otherwise the results could be disastrous. Start with a small project and give a very clear brief so that there's no scope for fighting over how the task should be approached. Review progress. Then it may be safe to give them shared responsibility for an important, difficult project. Send them on a business trip, for instance, or make them jointly responsible for planning the Christmas festivities. Time in each other's company can work wonders. The main aim is to encourage them to recognize their interdependence, by creating shared objectives, a common enemy, or a situation in which they must sink or swim together.

2. Personality / Style
When it's you…
Organizations populated by clones lack the variety needed to be successful. It's important to have a rich blend of different styles, skills and strengths. Unfortunately, differences are not always easily

tolerated. The important thing here is to understand a particular difference and its value, then make sure you are maximizing it to realize joint potential. It is not always entirely clear what the difference is, you may need help here. Talk to the person about your feelings and encourage them to give you feedback. Be honest, not only in terms of how they behave, but the impact that it has on you. Discuss each other's strengths, reach an understanding of how they can be used and agree how you will work together in the future. You may need assistance from an objective third party to help you see things from the other perspective.

When it's others...
When you see people clashing in this way, you may need to intervene to help them recognize the other's contribution. Give them feedback. Get them to give each other feedback. Use an impartial mediator if necessary. Ultimately, the individuals involved must learn how to deal with each other, and how to interpret what is being said.

3. Philosophy/Values
When it's you...
This is more difficult. Values and beliefs go right to the very centre of an individual's character. You are not going to change that. Nor are you likely to change your own to fit more neatly with their philosophy. Why would you want to, even if you could? All you can do is recognize the difference, believe with all your heart that they have just as much right to their values as you do to yours, and get on with getting on with them. You could then work with the person to agree how you should both modify your behaviours so that you can work more productively (see 2. Personality/Style above).

This becomes a different issue if one person is "right" and the other is "wrong". For instance, it may well be that you have a set of beliefs which is consistent with what the organization is striving for, while the other person clearly does not. When this is the case, it is often possible to point out instances when the "offender" has acted inappropriately and say why you think their behaviour was out of line. Talk to the individual – tell them your views. If that doesn't work, there may be a case for enlisting the support of your boss. Outline your case carefully, give examples to back it up and state how you have tried to address the situation. Be objective and avoid exaggeration.

When it's others…
If you are called in to deal with a case like this, it's essential to be impartial. More often than not, both philosophies are acceptable to the company – just not to each other! Here you have to look for common ground. What is it that they both agree on? Can this form the basis of a productive working relationship? Point out to them that people do have different values: one person might throw their heart and soul into getting to the top, while the other wants a more balanced lifestyle. These differences need to be accommodated – by the organization and by the individuals involved – if both are going to continue working for the company. Get them to think of ways in which they can plan and organize their work to get the most from each other. Then follow up and review the situation.

4. Conflict of interest
When it's you…
Frequently, with this type of conflict, the issue involved is organizational, not personal. In other words, the problem is caused by structure and process – not individual differences. The way many organizations are set up these days people can't help but compete. Project managers fighting for finance from a limited pot, or salespeople chasing a finite customer base, are good examples.

The solution here is one of compromise and "swings and roundabouts". Until the systems or processes change, this conflict will remain. So it's in your interest to talk to the individual concerned and agree how you can best work together. Remind them it's not personal, be open about the potential win–lose situation, and stress your desire for a compromise which is acceptable to both of you.

When it's others…
If you are charged with dealing with this type of breakdown, it could well be that you are talking about one team vs another.

Of course, the ideal situation is to change the system, improve the reward mechanism, so that people benefit from co-operating instead of competing. If that's not possible, try to alter the way they perceive the situation. Remind them of the principle of "you scratch my back, I'll scratch yours". Make them understand that co-operation is valued by your organization, it will be recognized – and ultimately rewarded – even if there is disappointment in the short term. Then be true to your word. (See Chapter 12 for more information on this.)

But often, there is a deeper conflict, which can't be removed by a change in the system. For example, the team responsible for maintaining computers will always hanker after stability, while those who design systems will always want change. Help each to understand the problems the other faces. Get them working together, focusing on higher level objectives and goals. Remind them that they are both needed. Beware of false dilemmas – the black and white thinking which leads us to insist on "either/or" solutions, when nine times out of ten compromise is possible.

5. Injury

When it's you...

If an individual has upset or hurt you, allowing it to fester will only store up trouble. You owe it to yourself to tell someone about it. The best person, if you can face it, is the person who caused the problem. In most situations, the culprit doesn't even realize they've done anything wrong. Just talking about it can clear up misunderstandings. However, they may be well aware of what they've done – and think they have a good reason for it. You need to know what that is. If you really can't face confronting the individual, then you should talk to your manager about the situation and they can take it forward. (If it's your manager who's hurt you, see Chapter 8 for advice.)

When it's others...

If you are a manager – or you are a friend who cares about what's happened and would like to help sort it out – you need to get to both parties quickly, otherwise the situation will deteriorate. There are nearly always two sides to the story. These need to be out in the open. Use an objective mediator – someone without an axe to grind. Let each person have their say and make the other listen. Allow them to talk it through. Summarize throughout. Then get them to come to some agreement on how to work together in the future. Make sure they know that you're going to follow this up. The ultimate aim here is to get people to forgive and forget – and ensure it doesn't happen again.

6. Prejudice

Prejudice is a word that is often used by people to describe a whole range of feelings and emotions connected to a fear and dislike of individuals who are different to us, or who don't fit into our idea of the norm. A prejudice is an unreasonable judgement based on little knowledge or experience of the individual or group of people concerned. Prejudices become harmful when they form the basis for negative action or behaviour against people. This then develops into discrimination – treating others unfairly because of something about themselves they cannot change, or that others dislike – often irrationally.

In an organizational context, discrimination can occur in all kinds of areas for all types of reasons. Traditionally we are aware of discrimination related to gender, race, sexual orientation and religion. Wider issues, such as age, class, geographical background, political allegiances and social status, are also reasons why people discriminate negatively. Regardless of the issue, discrimination in the workplace cannot be tolerated.

Discrimination, as recognised in UK legislation, normally takes three forms:

- Direct behaviour aimed at you specifically because of your sex, race or disabilities.
- Indirect systems, procedures, requirements or conditions which – whether intentional or not – have the impact of discriminating against you on sex, race or disability grounds.
- Victimization – further action against you because you have already made a complaint.

So what can you do if you feel you've been discriminated against? Talking to someone you can trust about your experience can help you focus on the type of action that you wish to take. There are several choices:

- Assertively challenging the perpetrator yourself.
- Asking a friend or colleague to help you confront the behaviour.
- Reporting the matter to your line manager or personnel department.
- Asking your union to intervene on your behalf.
- Taking it outside to an agency such as (in the UK) the Citizen's Advice Bureau, a solicitor, the Equal Opportunities Commission or the Commission for Racial Equality.

Whatever your choice of action, no-one needs to put up with discriminatory behaviour, and organizations have a responsibility to ensure we all work in a safe, positive environment.

When it's others…
This is perhaps the most tricky area. Prejudice is both difficult to prove, and to deal with. But it's essential to be alert to this type of conflict – especially if you are a manager – as you could find yourself with a lawsuit on your hands. Tread carefully. Explain how it appears to you – and to the other people involved – using examples to back up your case. Listen carefully. Make it clear that you won't tolerate discrimination on any grounds. Remind people of the law and company policy on equal opportunities. Say that you will be seeking feedback to see how the situation develops – from them, from the person who has drawn your attention to the situation, and from others who are in a position to observe what is happening. Then keep a close eye on things. The aim here is to create understanding and tolerance. It's not easy and it doesn't happen overnight. But exposing the problem can certainly speed this process up.

7. Jealousy
When it's you…
This too is a difficult area, since most people who are jealous of others will find all sorts of other reasons for their aversion. So the first thing you need to do is to acknowledge the real cause of your feelings. Remember that jealousy is a natural emotion and many people experience it. But at the same time be determined to do something about it. What precisely are you

envious of? Why? It's worth remembering that you have strengths too. Others could well be jealous of those. Tell yourself that this negative emotion is just not worthy of someone like you. It does no good at all. In fact, it can only be harmful. Wish the other person well and do your best to avoid being competitive.

When it's others…
If you have to deal with what you suspect to be jealousy in another person, explore it carefully with them. Try to get to the root cause. Remember that insecurity can cause these feelings, so make sure you let them know how much you value their strengths. Tell them that you consider them to be too good a performer and too much of an asset to allow jealousy to get in their way. Point out how much better they would be if they could conquer these undermining, unconstructive thoughts.

What are the principles for dealing with breakdowns?

You can try to work around a conflict: it's sometimes possible to arrange things so that the people who are at loggerheads never have to deal with each other. However, this is a laborious and hazardous approach, which leads to inefficiency and distraction. Innocent bystanders get involved and, of course, the basic problem remains. So it's far better to deal with the situation.

Ideally you would be able to foresee potential clashes and avoid them. However, it's inevitable that personal conflicts will arise from time to time. Here are some guidelines for dealing with them:

Nip trouble in the bud. Don't allow the situation to deteriorate by ignoring it and hoping it'll go away. The longer a dispute continues, the more difficult and painful it becomes to implement an effective solution.

Use an honest broker. People work through their problems faster with third party assistance. They may need help in getting the other person to listen or to understand how their own behaviour is coming across.

Don't rush to judgement. The blame is rarely all on one side. It's important that someone understands both sides of the story.

Assume the best motives. It's very easy to assume that people are deliberately being difficult and obstructive. Try to believe that both individuals mean well and that they are not digging their heels in for no reason at all.

Understand the reasons. Don't waste time picking off symptoms, the issues will just re-emerge in a different way. Take time to get to the heart of the matter.

Make the remedy fit the cause. Choose an appropriate way of dealing with the problem.

Follow up. This needs to happen regularly and over time. It's vital to prevent old wounds re-opening or hostilities resuming after an official cease-fire has been declared.

CHAPTER 8

Managing your boss

"I once worked as part of a small, very close knit team, which was managed by a dictatorial, lazy boss. She wouldn't accept criticism from us and it seemed that senior managers were too afraid to tackle her. One by one we came to hate her, our jobs, in fact anything to do with the organization. We became desperate to leave and ended up taking the first jobs offered – simply to escape the situation."

Introduction

One of the trickiest political challenges faced by many people at work is that of managing their boss. A difficult, unproductive relationship with a line manager is one of the greatest sources of stress to people – and it gets in the way of effective working. It may also be damaging to the team, both in terms of productivity and morale. In extreme instances, you find a department united against a common enemy – the boss – but that's just about the *only* positive knock-on effect that poor management can produce!

Given that, it's surprising how many individuals are reluctant to stand up to their boss and actively manage the situation: "Why should I manage my boss? Surely they're supposed to be managing me?" Or, worse still: "I'm scared to say anything because it could damage my career." This avoidance of the situation and failure to take any responsibility whatsoever is unproductive. The best that can happen is that the situation continues at the same level. In the worst case scenario, the situation deteriorates to a level that people just can't tolerate. They then leave.

Consider one thing: your boss may not even know that they are a demotivating manager. It's a fact of life that managers, at whatever level, do not get enough feedback from the people who report to them, for the reasons described above. So if your boss is unaware that they are doing anything wrong, what choice do they have but to continue in the same vein? So you have to take action – but it must be the *right* action. What is likely to work in your particular situation?

Defining the problem

First, you will need to isolate in your mind precisely what it is they do that has such a negative impact. The complaints that people make about their bosses generally fall into four categories. These are given below, along with examples of the extremes that you would expect to find under each heading.

Flexibility problems	Attitude problems
● Flexible vs rigid	● Trustworthy vs untrustworthy
● Listening vs telling	● Ethical vs unethical
● Compromising vs dogmatic	● Fair vs unfair
Developmental problems	**Competence problems**
● People focus vs task focus	● Organized vs chaotic
● Empowering vs controlling	● Effective vs ineffective
● Developmental vs repressive	● Credible vs lacking respect

This is by no means an exhaustive list, but it captures the most frequently made complaints about bosses. When it comes to managing the problems they can cause, you have to tailor your approach to your individual circumstance. However, there is an overall pattern which applies in most cases:

1. Define problem → 2. Identify cause → 3. Understand effect →
4. Agree remedy → 5. Review

In terms of stages 1, 2 and 3, the guidelines below may help you to clarify your thinking about your particular situation. Stages 4 and 5 are covered later in the chapter.

Understanding cause and effect

Flexibility problems

All the issues in this category are concerned with the extent to which your boss listens to others and takes their ideas on board – including accepting feedback about their own performance and behaviour. To be managed by a person who is completely inflexible can be frustrating, especially if you are someone full of ideas.

The first step in addressing the situation is to understand why your boss behaves in this way. Flexibility problems may stem from a lack of imagination. It could be that the individual concerned has been with the company for so many years that they wouldn't dream of doing it any other way than "the way we've always done it". Alternatively, it could be that they are naturally risk averse. This type of boss inevitably stifles creativity and runs the risk of missing out on opportunities for improvement. A department managed in this way will lag behind others in the innovation stakes and quickly get a reputation for being stuck in the mud. High flyers will, therefore, tend to avoid it.

The approach to handling – and ultimately changing – the situation is centered around **confidence building.** You slowly need to gain the trust of your manager and win them over to the notion that new/other people's ideas can be useful. The more they see success, and the more they benefit from it, the more likely they are to be up for innovation and change in the future.

At the other end of the scale, however, you get the boss who is *too* flexible – they blow with the wind/sit on the fence/lack the courage of their conviction. Again, you need to understand why they behave in this way. Is it caused by a complete inability to say "no" up the line? Do their bosses keep moving the goalposts? Or could it be that the individual has a genuinely open mind? Whatever the cause, this type of leadership too can cause havoc in the shape of errors, re-working and duplication. People in the team complain about a lack of direction and inconsistent leadership. Flexibility is one thing, but an unfocused team without an effective leader is quite another.

Dealing with this type of situation is all about **clarifying the brief.** The individual is not going to change overnight. However, you can make sure that the way you manage them minimizes unnecessary work. When they set you a task, make sure you have clearly understood both what is required of you and why. If it's not urgent, delay for a few days and then check back – is it still required? Give your boss feedback about this tendency to change the requirement, and the impact that has. Ask them about the reasons and be sympathetic. Monitor the situation and remember to give them credit as the situation stabilizes.

Attitude problems

This often boils down to two main issues:

- The extent to which your boss's attitudes and beliefs coincide with your own, those espoused by the organization, or those held by society as a whole.
- The way in which your boss utilizes formal or positional power. In other words, the power your boss has by virtue of their position in the company.

It may not matter that your boss has a different outlook on life from your own – as long as they are not imposing these views on you or refusing to listen to your perspective. However, your boss's influence is considerable and "pulling rank" is commonplace in organizational life. You can then find yourself the victim of an abuse of positional power. In determining how to deal with this problem, two factors are significant: the effect it's having on you, and whether others share your dissatisfaction.

If the problem is yours alone – i.e. the boss doesn't agree with your views – you need to challenge yourself: is it the case that one of you is right and one of you is wrong, or that both points of view have something to commend them, but the two are in conflict? Your argument will have more chance of prevailing if your boss is out of line with either the organization or society as a whole. But if it just comes down to your opinion versus theirs, it's a fact of business life that the boss's view generally carries more weight. That doesn't mean you shouldn't try, however. Chapters 5, 6 and 7 go into a great deal of depth on how to address this type of problem.

You are in a slightly stronger position if you find that your colleagues are also dissatisfied. It may be possible to collect feedback from the whole team to validate your own perceptions and – if necessary – to build a case.

In broad terms, dealing with the situation is all about **making your views known**. This needs to be done in a constructive way, pointing out the differences between their view and yours, and the impact that has. This should not be done in an aggressive way. Think about the encounter in terms of "problem solving", rather than "having an argument". If you have gathered together the views of other people, do not use this information as part of your opening gambit. "Ganging up", or the formation of a coalition, is not a particularly effective influencing technique. However, if you have tried to be constructive, adopted a problem solving approach and listened to your boss's point of view, and your boss *still* fails to listen, this kind of information can be a useful backup.

Above all, it's important to have a real desire to solve the problem. I recently worked with a team who were experiencing significant problems with their boss. The team had developed extremely close relationships with one another – united against a common enemy! They complained of such a lack of trust that they felt it was too late to recover the situation. When pushed, however, they admitted that they didn't actually want to try. They felt so hurt by the individual's behaviour that it was preferable for them to continue running mutual support sessions at the pub and generally snubbing their boss than it was to sort the situation out. Avoid this behaviour. It's always better to try to solve a problem, than it is to accommodate it – or even revel in it!

Developmental problems

These issues are all related to the extent to which your boss is interested in developing and stretching others. It's common sense that the more responsibility you can encourage the team to take, the more productive they will be, and research indicates that they are liable to be more motivated too. So why do so many bosses feel inclined to repress talent and keep people "in their place"?

One answer is that they are insecure in themselves. They are not confident in their own abilities and the way they deal with that is to keep reminding people about how untouchable *they* are in terms of performance – especially since they have such a poor bunch of people working for them. Others are rarely fooled, however.

By stark contrast, people who are confident in their own abilities tend to be only too pleased to see the team excelling. They recognize that the success of their people is a credit to their leadership abilities. Instead of clinging on to their top performers, they are delighted to see them promoted out of the team because they are confident that they will become ambassadors elsewhere in the organization.

Alternatively, it could be that the boss is so task focused, that people don't even come into the equation: "What do you mean, I have to coach and empower my people? I haven't got time to do that – I've got work to do!" This too is surprisingly common. The number of managers who talk about the "people stuff" as distinct from "the real job" is shocking. There is some evidence, however, that this is changing – albeit slowly.

A third possible cause could be that the individual is risk averse and a bit of a control freak! This could be driven by a lack of trust in the ability of others and the belief that "I can do this better than you ever could".

Whatever the cause of the problem, the result is always the same – people do not develop and grow. Not, that is, unless they take the initiative themselves.

This restricts the impact that the whole team can have and the best people become fed up and leave. In addition, the boss doesn't grow either. They carry on doing the same job month in month out – a job that is probably *at least* a level below the one they're being paid to do.

Dealing with the issue is all about **demanding what you're entitled to**. Because many managers do not consider the development of others to be a fundamental part of their role, their direct reports too consider personal development to be a luxury. They become nervous about asking for support, guidance and coaching, because they fear it will be seen as wasting their boss's time. Don't be afraid to ask. Couch your request in terms of how much better you will be able to serve the department, how much greater your productivity will be – in other words, make sure they know what's in it for them.

If you suspect that their motivation for suppressing others is a lack of security on their part, point out to them that developing others is a part of their managerial role. A strong, well-trained team will be a credit to them and a sign of their success.

Don't shy away from this one. The more you ask for development, the more you get, the more others follow your lead, and the more your boss will become accustomed to fulfilling this part of their role.

Competence problems

At the extreme end of the scale, you have a boss who is inefficient, ineffective and unrespected. Unlucky for you if your manager is all three! But hopefully you will be able to isolate the problem in just one of these areas. A lack of organization can be due to ignorance – the individual genuinely doesn't know how to organize their time and the workload. But more frequently, it's a question of will. How many people do you know who have been on time management courses, but still seem disorganized and panicky? Most people know the theory, it's just a question of putting it into practice. In his book *First Things First*, Stephen Covey, the well-known American management writer, talks about the psychopathology known as "urgency addiction": a complete inability to get excited about anything until the deadline is looming! This is a common phenomenon at all levels of an organization.

Linked with this is the ability to get results – the effectiveness vs ineffectiveness continuum. The reasons for this could be numerous: lack of training, lack of experience, or even lack of confidence. It may also be caused by problems in the other categories, for example, an unwillingness to develop other people, leading to an inability to delegate.

Then there's the issue of credibility – again linked. Clearly, if your boss doesn't get things done – or gets them done, but always late and in a sloppy manner – others will not have respect for them. Alternatively, it could be that your boss does not respect others: a lack of respect for another individual will often provoke the same feeling in return.

Dealing with this type of situation is linked to **giving feedback**. Put yourself in your boss's shoes. If you were in their position, how would you like to receive the feedback? Plan your approach on the basis of that. Your boss can then decide how they want to deal with the situation. In certain circumstances, it may be appropriate for you to do some upward coaching (see below). Do it! Coaching doesn't have to follow hierarchical rules.

Agreeing the remedy

So you have defined the problem in your own mind, you have considered why the individual might behave in that manner, and you have thought about the impact that their behaviour has – on you, the team, and the business. In short, you have prepared your case. But how do you go about agreeing the remedy? There are a number of principles you need to adhere to:

- Pick the right time and place – in private, when you both have the time to dedicate to the issue.
- Be empathetic – just because this person is your boss, it doesn't mean to say they don't have feelings too – put yourself in their shoes.
- Give a balanced view – state what you do like about their approach, not just what you don't like.
- Remember at all times that you want to solve the problem.
- Listen to their point of view.
- Be open about the way in which you like to be treated – and explain why.
- Be constructive.
- Offer your suggestions for solutions – don't just present problems.
- Be on the lookout for non-verbal signals, which may indicate that you don't really have their attention or agreement to the fact there's a problem. Examples of this include a failure to make eye contact, an inability to concentrate, general impatience, nodding and agreeing when you don't really feel they're interested, and a lack of listening.
- If appropriate, summarize actions and make sure they agree.

- Work to get their agreement for you – and others – to give them feedback about how well they are doing on an ongoing basis.

Using these principles, it may be appropriate for you to coach your boss. Don't position the meeting as such: it could appear to be presumptuous, patronizing or just plain inappropriate. But you can be in the driving seat – subtly and productively!

Upward coaching

- Set the context: what you are trying to achieve and why.
- Give your feedback: outline how your boss's behaviour impacts on you and/or the team.
- Ask for their response to that and their perspective on things.
- Agree what needs to change/be achieved. Don't rush this stage. If you don't mutually agree what the problem is and the desired outcome, any further work on planning action will be a waste of time.
- Discuss how things might be changed: don't impose solutions or give your advice without first seeking their views. Listen to them carefully. Build on their ideas, making it clear that it is their thinking, not yours.
- Confirm actions: what needs to be done, by whom and when.

What is all important is the way in which this process is managed. In planning for this meeting, be sure to check Chapters 5 and 7 as there is helpful information about giving feedback and dealing with difficult situations.

Reviewing the result

Once you have tackled a particular issue, it is necessary to review the results and maintain the dialogue. Remember that behaviours don't transform themselves overnight, and there are usually hiccups. (Personal change is difficult – think about the last time you made a commitment to change your habits!) It is essential to reinforce behaviours that demonstrate your boss is making an effort and also to give feedback when they are slipping back into their old ways.

Once a specific issue seems to be resolved, you are then into a maintenance situation. In other words, there is a need to ensure that the relationship continues to be satisfactory and there's no back-sliding – on either part! Bear in mind, however, that people can revert to type, especially under pressure. Don't assume that the backward step has become a trend! But don't be complacent and do nothing either. There are a number of general principles that apply during this maintenance period:

- Do your bit.
- Help your boss to do their bit.
- Maintain an open relationship.
- Learn to say no – but remember that they too have the right to turn down your suggestions.

Do your bit

Despite having tackled the big issues, there will inevitably be day-to-day niggles. If something does seem to be going wrong, try, just for a minute, putting yourself into your boss's shoes. Why are they behaving like this today? What pressures and concerns are they likely to have? What work (and home) related problems could be grinding them down? Are *you* doing something to make the situation worse? How will they be feeling as a result?

This can often be a tricky exercise, especially if they are really getting on your nerves! But thinking it through will help you to understand where your boss is coming from and, therefore, what they might want from you. Help to defuse the situation by trying to work in a way which will make their life easier. Be positive: instead of coming up with 100 reasons why something *can't* be done, focus on how you *could* make it work. Be realistic about what can be delivered – *over*, rather than *under*-estimate timescales – and deliver what you promise.

Help your boss to do their bit

You now have some credit in the bank. You are being supportive, empathetic and helping to get things done. You need to make sure they understand how to do the same in return. This is all about ongoing feedback.

Think carefully about what you want them to do differently. Be selective and focused: most people find it depressing and difficult to listen to an endless list of personal flaws. Your message is more likely to be heard if you pick on one or two key areas and concentrate on those.

Think through how you are going to give this feedback. Your boss will be more inclined to acknowledge the negative points if you have first told them what you actually like about their style. Acknowledge your own faults and suggest things you can do to improve. Most importantly, explain your motivation. This is not about you having a nicer or an easier time at work, it's about how you can be more effective and provide a better service. Of course, you will enjoy work more, but what's wrong with a win-win situation?

Finally, don't make too big a deal of it. If you are very tense and blunder the situation, it is likely to sound like a huge issue. By contrast, if you are informal and relaxed – but still assertive – the message will be far more palatable, and likely to get through.

Maintain an open relationship

Good working relationships take time to develop. You will need to maintain an open dialogue with your boss – keeping them informed about what's going on in your work and showing an interest in theirs. If there's a problem, don't let it fester. Let them know quickly and try to have your solution ready. Make it easy for them to help you to help them.

Learn to say no

Remember, nine times out of ten your focus should be positive. But you do need to know where to draw the line. If you overload yourself, you run the risk of damaging your overall performance, not to mention your state of mind! So there will be times when you just have to say no.

Learn to do it in the right way. Outline all the other tasks you currently have on your plate and ask which of these they are prepared to let slip. Alternatively, suggest someone else who might be able to do the job and offer to brief them. Always present yourself as someone who *solves* rather than creates problems.

When all else fails

Finally, there are situations in which, despite having given it your very best shot, you still cannot develop a productive working relationship with your boss, and the conflict continues. The example given at the very start of this chapter was one such scenario. In that example, the whole team left the company one by one. But before taking such drastic steps, you may think about going to a higher authority.

If you have first made every reasonable effort to remedy the situation, and you can state quite clearly what you have done on this front, the senior manager is likely to give you a sympathetic hearing. But be prepared, your immediate boss will inevitably be called in to account for their actions. And once that's happened, they are likely to want to have a conversation with you! You need to be prepared for this – both psychologically and organizationally. In advance, work through the following process:

Prepare an approach

- What is the desired outcome in terms of:
  - your feelings?
  - your boss's feelings?
  - the impression you've created?
  - future working arrangements?
- How are you most likely to achieve that outcome?
- What will definitely get in the way?
- How, therefore, should you approach the meeting?

Prepare a defence

- What are the facts of the current situation?
- What is the history?
- What steps have you taken to address the situation?
- How have those efforts been received by your boss?
- What caused you to approach your senior manager?

Prepare yourself

- Are you happy with the efforts you made to address the situation before you approached the senior manager?
- If yes: you did everything you felt able to at the time and you were well within your rights to escalate the issue.
- If no: perhaps you will need to acknowledge you could have done more, but you were still well within your rights.
- Prepare yourself to take an assertive approach: how can you avoid being aggressive, apologetic or passive?
- Breathe deeply and try to relax as much as you can.

How you begin will depend upon the approach your boss decides to adopt. They may well be apologetic and seem determined to solve the situation. However, the safest assumption to make is that that won't happen! It is more likely that they will start the meeting by demanding an explanation from you, in which case you will need to use the defence that you prepared in advance.

Outline your views carefully and calmly, all the time trying to maintain eye contact and an assertive approach. You should then ask for your boss's viewpoint on the situation, and listen and respond appropriately. Remember, even if you are initially forced onto the back foot, all is not lost – you can still persist with the more constructive approach that you also prepared in advance. You just need to use your judgement to gauge how useful it would be in the circumstances.

Escalating the matter may feel like an extreme measure, but it can often be what is required to sort the problem out – kill or cure, as they say!

CHAPTER 9

Putting communication to work

A large financial services organization had just gone through a merger. People from both companies were nervous about what was going to happen, and distrustful of the "other side". This suspicion started at the top – the directors, too, feared for their jobs and felt the need to compete with their peers. But despite these frictions, the board understood the need to communicate with "the troops", and so put out a message assuring people that the future would be focused on development – both of individuals and of the business. On the face of it, a transparent and encouraging message. But by the time it had filtered through to the "front line" it had turned into a coded message for redundancy. This is a very vivid illustration of the fact that it's not *what* you say, it's *how* you say it and the *actions* which accompany the message that matter.

Introduction

What is politics if it's not about communication? Conveying a message, swaying opinion and making sure that people are coming around to your way of thinking is the main aim of all political activity. And it's as true in the world of office politics as it is in the arena of national or local politics. Office politicians pride themselves on having an ear to the ground and always being well informed about what's going on – right through from board level to the more subversive cliques. They use the information gleaned selectively – and sometimes manipulatively – to achieve their ends. And they are quick to read the results and interpret the impact. Communication is the mainstay of their political lives.

Communication for office politicians

So let's think about communication as it applies to the office politician:

- **Reading the runes.** All good office politicians will tell you that you are naïve to believe what you're told. *They* dig deeper. They spend their lives interpreting both what they're hearing, and what they're not hearing. Nothing wrong with that, apart from the fact that they frequently make two plus two equal seven! As a consequence, they can find their logic flawed, their actions based on false assumptions and their behaviour becoming increasingly paranoid.

- **Storing up information.** The office politician works on the basis that "information is power" – the more they know that others don't, the stronger their position. Of course, it's no good merely possessing the knowledge, others have to know – or, better still, suspect – that they possess it! So they allude to the fact that they're in the know, while apologizing for being unable to share the information with you.

- **Selective leaking.** If it's in their interest, office politicians will not shy away from sharing their booty with appropriate receivers. They may choose trustworthy individuals so that they themselves can enjoy the pleasure of serial disclosure. Alternatively, they may want the story to be widely known, in which case they use people who are notoriously leaky, emphasizing the extreme sensitivity of the material and the imperative need to ensure that it goes no further, thereby guaranteeing that the "secret" will be public knowledge within hours!

- **Using what they know.** In terms of the accuracy of their communication, office politicians are liable to operate at either end of a continuum – all good news, or all bad news. If you are in a position of seniority, or relative power, they are liable to tell you precisely what you want to hear. With others, they can be brutally frank. This is usually positioned as being in the best interest of the recipient – "you've got to be cruel to be kind" – and blame for the indictment or allegation is often placed elsewhere. The office politician does, after all, want to be loved and/or respected.

This approach to communication is not an ideal role model to follow. It is unreliable, wastes time and can be damaging. However, it is important to understand how these characters and the other informal communications mechanisms operate before you can get a real grip on how you *should* be doing it.

We can't move on, therefore, without a discussion of the dreaded grapevine!

The grapevine

It's a sad indictment that – after years of corporate initiatives to improve internal communications – employee opinion surveys still tend to reveal that people receive most information via the grapevine. Their stated preference is usually to be informed, face-to-face, by their line manager. So why does the grapevine continue to be such a success (in prevalence, if not in accuracy)? Well let's look at the alternative first. Most formal communications mechanisms still tend to be:

- One-way: the transmission of a message with no feedback and no interaction.
- One direction: top down or centre out.
- Factual: expressed in a logical way with no accounting for emotion or feelings.
- Superficial: too little real information or analysis to be of relevance to individuals, or...
- Overly complex: *all* the details, *all* the complexity (used typically when no-one could really be interested or understood the subject).
- Generic: the same information to everyone – a sheep dip.
- Systems or paper based: hundreds of memos and e-mails, circulated pretty much randomly.

Characteristics

This doesn't describe all organizations' approach to communications, but it does account for many. And it's fair to say that *most* companies could do with some improvement in this area. We have to be careful though. Many specialists consider "internal communications" to be a convenient scapegoat: they believe that responsibility for complaints often belongs elsewhere. But keeping this health warning in mind, let's see how formal systems compare with the ever-flourishing grapevine. The grapevine has a number of distinctive characteristics:

- It's timely – managers are shocked at the speed with which a message can permeate the whole organization.
- It's relevant – you don't bother passing things on if you can't see their relevance, either to you or to the recipient. The grapevine usually occupies itself with things that people want to hear about.
- It's personal – there is normally a face-to-face element. Having said that, the "e-grapevine" is rapidly becoming a part of working life! But these are not blanket, widely circulated missives, as the formal e-mails tend to be, which probably accounts for their success.
- It's tailored – if you pass on a message, you're going to make sure that it has relevance for the receiver. You think therefore about what you are going to say, the impact you want to have, and you tailor your message and delivery to make sure it hits the spot.
- It's multi-directional – the grapevine is not constrained by formal reporting lines or organizational structures. It goes beyond these traditional boundaries, which is why a message can very quickly be conveyed to a whole organization, while more formal mechanisms struggle to get that penetration.
- It's discursive – you don't just deliver the message and then go away again, you want to hear the person's response and give your own perspective. It's all about debate, not transmission. And feedback loops are built in, so the chances are you'll go back to the person who told you and let them know how people are responding.

Because the grapevine has these characteristics, it may be tempting to use it as a method of communication. Furthermore, its appeal is intensified because it's unofficial, easy to deny, and effortlessly manipulated. But this would be a serious mistake.

Don't forget that there are also a lot of damaging and negative characteristics of the grapevine. It often paints a blacker picture than the situation requires, and its inaccuracy is notorious. In addition, managers who use the grapevine can lose respect. People perceive them as gossips, scaremongers or even cowards – scared to address the team honestly, openly and face-to-face.

Instead of using the grapevine, it would be far better to look at its positive characteristics and build these into a more formal system, such as team briefing. Certainly, more enlightened organizations do indeed make sure that their communications channels are timely, relevant, personal, tailored, multi-directional and discursive. And, as a result, they witness a huge increase in understanding and awareness, and a comparable reduction in grapevine activity.

Getting it wrong

We have dwelt so long on how *not* to communicate purely because so many companies – and individuals – still regularly get it wrong. And the impact can be devastating. Take the case study below for instance.

Case study A financial services organization was planning to relocate its head office to a nearby location – just ten miles down the road. There would be no redundancies, but inevitably some people would face a longer journey to work – or even need to move house. The decision was communicated as follows.

At lunch time, on the last Thursday before Christmas, the following e-mail was sent by the chief executive to "all head office staff":

"You are required to attend a head office staff meeting at 3.30pm tomorrow. Please cancel any prior arrangements – either internal or external.
Signed..."

On receiving this e-mail, everyone stopped work. There had never been a meeting of all head office staff before. What was it all about? For the next four hours, people wandered around the office asking others if they'd seen the message and what they thought it was all about. At 5.30pm many went to the pub.

The next day at work was a similar story: fear, anticipation, speculation. By the time the meeting arrived, most had already made up their minds what it was about – redundancy.

At the meeting, you could have cut the atmosphere with a knife. People read significance into the layout of the seats, who was present and who was going to address them. If anyone was missing, they had theories about that too. Most were in such a state by the start of the meeting that they were unable to listen to what was being said. They *didn't hear* the reassuring message about no redundancies. What they did hear, however, was the need for each individual to book a meeting for the following week to discuss their personal position. There were only two working days to go until the Christmas break.

With this hanging over them, pretty much everyone had a bad weekend. They found it difficult to concentrate on anything other than their potential fate at work. They wished they already knew what would happen to them, instead of having to wait until their meeting the next week. The fact that Christmas was almost upon them just reinforced the black mood.

It has to be said that this is a long way from being one of the *worst* examples of corporate communication: it was well-planned, leak-free, and the news wasn't *that* bad. But the negative impact was significant.

So what should they have done differently? First, they could have put people's minds at rest. If you can honestly deny the worst case scenario – do so. In advance of a merger, a London insurance company recently announced that there would be *no* compulsory redundancies. This was the first communication to people. Some of the senior management team thought it was crazy to raise the subject at all. But they were proved wrong. The reassurances did the trick.

In the case study above, the chief executive could have done the same and made it clear in the advance e-mail that the meeting was *not* to announce redundancies. This would have relaxed the staff and made them far more receptive to the real message.

Many people fall into this trap. They think that to reveal information in advance will lessen its impact on the day. What they should be thinking about is how they can make the message more effective – and humane.

In addition, the timing of the announcement could have been better. Best practice dictates that you don't give bad news on a Friday afternoon, or before public holidays. People tend to get even more depressed when the weekend or holiday spirit seems rife elsewhere. It can be a very lonely time – the people at home don't really understand the situation and you feel guilty about them. Suicide rates peak at weekends and holiday periods. It is far better to give the news in the middle of the week, when people have a chance to talk it through – perhaps with their colleagues.

Two small errors – but both had a significant impact. And it's these things that you need to anticipate and do your utmost to avoid – both at a corporate level and as an individual. How many times have you been cross with yourself for putting your foot in it? How many times have you been surprised when a seemingly innocuous comment has been taken out of all proportion? Getting it right takes thought, time and effort.

Getting it right

First of all, you need to decide if you are a **leader** or a **follower.** Most professional politicians follow. If your key objective is re-election, and all you really want to do is stay in power, it is always tempting to adopt a populist approach.

Company life differs in that the logic of the bottom line – and the visible and rapid link between action and results – should be the most powerful driver of behaviour. The most successful people in organizations are usually ahead of the game, but not *too* far ahead. Woody Allen always says that you should turn up to the cinema 15 minutes before the feature is due to be screened. If you arrive an hour early, no-one will know what to do with you, and if you're late, they won't let you in! This applies equally to business. Stay a little bit ahead and people will consider you inspiring – but not wacky! That does *not* mean to say you shouldn't be ambitious in your goals. It merely suggests that you should take a steady approach to the way you communicate them. This will ensure you don't lose people along the way.

Who's who

Once you have made up your mind about whether to lead or follow, you need to understand the **who's who** of corporate life. This often has less to do with official hierarchies and reporting lines than with informal networks and power bases. Effective communicators understand these. They have an instinct for knowing who needs to know what and how they should be informed. You too should aim to develop this understanding and aptitude. Key people to watch for are as follows:

- **Opinion formers.** Spot them by the degree of influence they exert over what happens – irrespective of their position in the organization. These people are important and you should aim to develop effective relationships with them. This does not mean you have to kowtow to them and agree with everything they say, but it's useful for you to know the way they are thinking, and why. It is also good to have their ear, so that you are able to influence them.
- **Gatekeepers.** These are the people who seem to control the information flows in a company. Again, this may not be a function of their official role, but more to do with their belief that "information is power" – and that power is there for the taking! They open and close channels of communication, they control the speed with which information is revealed, and they filter/translate the details according to the message they need to convey. Be aware of their existence and their potential power. Use them wisely. Don't tell them things if you think they will misuse the information; but seek information from them. These people have significantly less power when communications channels are transparent and effective. You can help to bring about this situation.
- **Repositories.** These people have a wealth of knowledge and information, built up either through experience, or by keeping a constant ear to the ground. Don't hesitate to consult them.

Their word may not be gospel, but it could help to inform your decision-making process.

- **Cliques.** These are the informal groupings which inevitably develop in any organization. They may be thrown together by common interest – officially or unofficially. It could be something as simple as the fact they are all smokers, thrown together on the doorstep at break times. Cliques can represent an invaluable source of information, but be aware of any group prejudices.

These people change all the time and so the situation is never static. However, it may be a useful exercise for you to map out where you see the power and the various sources of information in your organization:

- Use a large sheet of paper and draw your immediate organization chart in the centre. Leave plenty of space around the chart.
- Then add to the chart anyone who impacts on you and your team. This may be your ultimate boss, or it could be people in other departments.
- Review the chart and mark against individuals whether you consider them to be opinion formers, gatekeepers or repositories. (NB: they may not be any of these!)
- Mark in a colour the individuals you consider to have the real power inside and outside the team.
- In another colour, add any informal lines of communication and mark any cliques of which you are aware.

Review the result. Are there people here you've been neglecting to talk to? Have you been as effective as you might in terms of tapping into the power bases in order to sound out ideas and get things agreed? Have you been ignorant of informal groupings that have been evolving? What do you need to do to address the situation? Why would you bother?

This last point is important. You will only be an effective communicator if you truly want to. If you can't see what's in it for you, then you are likely to continue as you always have done.

Once you've identified whom you need to talk to, it's important to communicate well. We talked earlier about doing your utmost to avoid putting your foot in it. This can be achieved by thinking through your message – and anticipating potential sensitivities – in advance. Think more broadly than you are used to doing. Who else would really benefit from this knowledge? The best way of getting information is to give it. If you make yourself useful to others, they are likely to return the favour.

Planning

The most important part of your preparation is to plan the impact you want to have. It's a well-known statistic that only 7% of the message conveyed in your verbal communication is down to the words you use. The remaining 93% is all associated with the *way* you say it and your body language. But most of us, when preparing for a presentation or talk, only think through what we're going to say. Instead, you should start with the impact you want to have: how do you want the individual(s) to think, feel and act once you have communicated with them? How are you most likely to achieve that result? Once you are clear about that, use the following checklist to plan what you want to say.

Purpose: *What do I want this communication to achieve?*

Who: *Who will be receiving this communication?*

What: *What information is to be communicated?*

Why: *Why is it necessary to communicate this information?*

How: *By what method is this information to be communicated?*

Where: *Where will this communication take place? (if applicable)*

When: *Is there a deadline for sending or receiving this communication?*

Action: *What needs to be done now?*

Following is a **worked example**.

Briefing of new team structure

I need to communicate the new team structure. The impact I want to have is for the audience to understand the implications, to know why the changes are happening, to be committed to the new structure, and to be motivated about the prospect of putting it into practice. The best way of doing that is a face-to-face briefing – all together – so that everyone receives the same information and has the opportunity to share thoughts, ideas and concerns. So…

Purpose:	*What do I want this communication to achieve?*	<ul><li>To communicate details of the new structure.</li><li>To outline actions and timescales.</li><li>To generate enthusiasm and commitment.</li><li>To collect ideas.</li><li>To answer concerns.</li></ul>
Who:	*Who will be receiving this communication?*	<ul><li>My team.</li><li>Administrative support.</li></ul>
What:	*What information is to be communicated?*	<ul><li>The fact that the changes *do not* mean redundancies, but opportunities for all.</li><li>An organization chart showing the new client-focused structure.</li><li>The rationale for the change: – to gain advantage over the competition – to enhance customer service – to provide more opportunities for career development and flexible working.</li><li>How people will be selected for the team leader and client manager roles.</li><li>Training and development available to people.</li><li>Key dates and specific actions.</li></ul>
Why:	*Why is it necessary to communicate this information?*	<ul><li>To inform people.</li><li>To quash the rumours that have been circulating.</li><li>To send the same message to everyone at the same time.</li><li>To put people's minds at rest.</li></ul>

		• To provide people with an opportunity to ask questions. • To get feedback.
How:	*By what method is this information to be communicated?*	• Short presentation. • 15 minutes for initial questions. • Ten minutes in groups of three to discuss: – their response – what it will mean for them in practice – any further questions – ideas and suggestions. • Feedback – five minutes from each team of three. • Discussion about next steps (15 minutes).
Where:	*Where will this communication take place?*	• In Conference Room A.
When:	*Is there a deadline for sending or receiving this communication?*	• Yes! Week ending 15 March, to allow enough time to implement the new structure before 1 May.
Action:	*What needs to be done now?*	• Design presentation and check with senior management. • Anticipate potential concerns and find answers to those questions. • Draft invitations to people, including the fact that this is an exciting opportunity for all. • Have invitations checked. • Send out invitations. • Practise presentation (checking for tone of voice, etc). • Book Conference Room A. • Order food and drinks for session.

Communication is the lifeblood of any organization. Ironically – or maybe because of this – it also tends to be a significant area of dissatisfaction. People are highly critical of a company's inability to communicate effectively. They complain about the lack – or overload – of information and the way in which news is transmitted.

But it's important to bear in mind that, no matter how good the company's communications processes and systems are, it's people who are responsible for administering those systems and it's people who are the recipients. Organizations are only effective at communicating if the individuals within those organizations are good at communicating. If you enhance your skills in this area and encourage others to do the same, the overall impact will go far beyond your own development.

CHAPTER 10

Making networks work for you

> "Office politics is all about recognizing and using informal power networks – both inside the organization and outside. In our company, two groups of people had different views about the best way forward for a part of the business. Group B out-manoeuvred Group A by using personal relationships at a senior level to overrule Group A's proposal."
> **Anonymous response to Office Politics Survey, Nicholson McBride, 1998**

Introduction

The last chapter was concerned with personal communication – both formal and informal. How can you most effectively find out about, and pass on, the things that matter?

In this chapter, we home in on an aspect of communication which is becoming increasingly important in the business world: networking.

When you mention networking, many people become sceptical, and some bitter. Images of the golf course, or the old school tie, pop graphically into their minds. And they remember the time when they were passed over for promotion, or weren't given a vital piece of information, just because they weren't "in with the in crowd". "It's not what you know, but who you know," they'll say.

In fact, the traditional "old boy" syndrome is becoming less significant. Today's networks assume different shapes. Succeeding in business these days still means forging and maintaining a wide range of strategic relationships, but there is a far wider choice available than just having had the good fortune to be at the "right" school.

What are networks?

Networks are simply groups of acquaintances – people you know, or know of. Nothing very sinister in that! At the most informal end of the scale, they are individuals you might pass the time of day with, bump into at the company social club, see at parents' evening, or whatever. As networks become more formal, there tends to be some common interest or agenda, a sporting connection for example. It could be that trade union membership brings you together. Or it may be that you are both like-minded individuals, interested in bringing about change in the organization, and keen to keep each other informed about what is happening.

If you ask people to draw their own personal network, most would come up with a **hub** diagram. They would be placed at the centre – the hub – and their connections would be arranged around them.

This, however, is a pretty primitive way of viewing a network. What about the people our contacts know, that we don't? We need to think on a broader basis than we have done in the past. This means that we start to bolt a series of **loop** and **branch** formations onto our basic network.

People who are effective networkers do this naturally. They recognize that they are *not* the centre of the universe and that their indirect contacts could be of as much interest as their direct contacts. They focus their efforts on understanding these connections, what use they might be, and how they might most effectively tap into them.

The final pattern to consider is the **club** formation. This, as the name suggests, is a group of people, all of whom know one

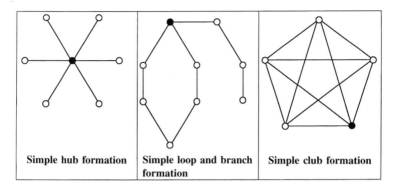

| Simple hub formation | Simple loop and branch formation | Simple club formation |

another. The different types of network are all represented graphically above. The shaded dot is you! The other dots are contacts – both direct and indirect.

Your network

Take a large sheet of paper. Draw yourself in the middle of it. Then start to build up a picture of your own network. Place the people you feel have significant influence over you close to you in the centre, and those with less influence slightly further out. Include within the diagram those people who are external to your organization, as well as those within it. Perhaps you could use different coloured dots for direct colleagues, people in other departments and external acquaintances? Once you have done this, join yourself to each of the contacts. Along these adjoining lines, write the nature of the connection and the influence they have over you. Then add the influence you have over them! Be imaginative and don't let false modesty get in the way of good analysis. Next to individuals' names, make a note of how the contact *could* be of interest. This need not be mercenary or selfish. It may well be that they could be useful to your team, or indeed, you may be able to help them out in some way. Finally, add in any relationships that they have with each other but which you are not involved with.

Review

Review the whole picture. What is the ratio of internal to external contacts? What does this mean? Are you too internally focused? If so, you may run the risk of limiting your horizons.

Or do you sit at the other end of the scale, with most of your contacts outside the company? The impact of this might be that you are not seen to be as interested in the organization as you might be; others are getting the upper hand, and you are unwittingly setting a ceiling on your career potential with your current employer. The impact is only worrying if it gets in the way of your aspirations. If you do want to be successful internally, you need to behave in a way which suggests to others – throughout the organization – that you have the interest, the aptitude and the expertise. Alternatively, you may be far more concerned about a future outside the company, in which case, the approach would be different.

This brings us to an important aspect of effective networking – it needs to have a purpose. There are only a certain number of hours in the day. You've seen from your diagram that your network is already huge – and complex. And that could be without really trying! If you were to attempt to develop and maintain meaningful, strategic relationships with everyone on that map, you would have little time for anything else. Forget about a home life! So you need to be clear about what you're doing it for.

Why network?

There are four basic reasons why people network:
● Information.
● Interest.
● Profile.
● Opportunity.

Information

The **information** category is all about keeping up-to-date with what's going on. You can tap into the latest thinking, or find someone to act as a sounding board for your own ideas.

Membership of this type of network will give you a broader perspective and could provide you with a wealth of information, which might make you a useful person to know back at the ranch. As well as face-to-face contact, this particular type of network also lends itself extremely well to Internet- or intranet-based systems.

Interest

The **interest** network aims to do something more than simply share facts and ideas amongst its membership. Of course, information will be a key element, but members of this type of network are focused on achieving common goals. These may be general aims and objectives, like a professional body working to advance the industry and maintain standards. Or they may be very specific targets – the anti-fox-hunting lobby in the UK aiming to bring about a total ban, for instance. Typically, these networks will be club shaped, although you will be able to identify examples of the other formations that fall into this category, most notably, the underground cliques which exist in many organizations.

Profile

Profile networks tend to be personal – being seen in the right places, making contact with the right people, and so on. But they could equally be about enhancing the status of a team or project. Some people consider this type of profile-raising activity to be highly unfair, even immoral. But it's a fact of life that senior managers have an enormous number of direct and indirect reports. As a consequence, they tend to remember only a few. It is those people who volunteer for projects, approach work proactively and make things happen who are more memorable. The results are obvious.

Opportunity

Finally, **opportunity** networks are the mainstay of business success. They involve establishing clearly what you want for the future – short, medium and long term – and identifying people who will be able to assist you in achieving your aspirations. Few senior positions are filled with respondents to newspaper advertisements. Most go to existing contacts, some of which may have been made relatively recently. And in these days of relationship marketing, new business comes less through cold calling, and more through word of mouth recommendation and personal relationships. It really is who you know that will make a difference to your business effectiveness. But don't worry:

opportunity networks can be developed, even if you weren't at Yale or Oxford! It just requires some forethought and application.

Are you a natural?

Are you one of those people who always seems to "know a man who can"? Or are you someone who merely observes this type of behaviour, wondering where on earth they've managed to drag that contact up from? Like many things in life, some people are naturals, and others aren't. Answer the questions below to find out if networking comes naturally to you.

Put a tick in either the True or False column, then calculate your score.

	True	False	Score
1. I am quick to pick up the phone.			
2. I feel very stimulated by anything new.			
3. I like to work things out for myself.			
4. I get bored rather easily.			
5. I always read about who's doing what in the newspaper.			
6. I prefer to write to people than phone them.			
7. I'm not scared to ask for support from people.			
8. I'm always introducing people to each other.			
9. My daily contact with people is limited to a few close colleagues.			
10. I quickly take advantage of new opportunities.			
11. At parties, I'm always fascinated to hear about what others do.			
12. I feel uncomfortable asking for favours.			
13. I'm always on the lookout for new ideas.			
14. I really enjoy getting out and about.			
15. I would describe myself as an introvert.			
Total			

For questions **1, 2, 4, 5, 7, 8, 10, 11, 13** and **14**, score yourself two points for every "true" answer and zero for a "false" answer.

For the remaining questions – **3, 6, 9, 12** and **15** – score two points for every "false" answer and zero for "true" answers.

The maximum score is 30 and if you are anywhere near this mark you are a true networker. In fact, any score of over 20 is pretty good. A total of ten to 20 is OK, but you should examine any statement for which you scored zero and think about the implications. Fewer than ten suggests that networking is really not up your street at all. However, even the most introverted can make progress in this area, provided they want to, and as long as they do it in a way which is consistent with their personality and values.

How to do it

First of all, you need to have a clear idea of what it is you want to achieve. This will point you in the direction of the most appropriate people. Make sure you act well in advance. The development of a good business relationship takes time. You need to start gently and develop mutual trust, respect and interest. And even if it's a small favour or piece of advice you're after, people won't thank you for putting pressure on them at the last minute.

Planning

Then plan. There are two elements to the planning process:

- What impression do you want to make?
- What are you going to say/do?

Your impression

First think about the impression you're going to make. If you feel in any way uncomfortable about what you're doing, this discomfort is likely to come through loud and clear. It is important to be positive about the contact and to think about it in terms of being mutually beneficial. When was the last time that someone asked you for help or advice? How did you feel about it? Flattered? Only too pleased to help? Bear in mind that most other people feel the same way.

Don't pin all your hopes on one contact. If you're not desperate, you won't sound it! Remember you're not asking for a job, or begging for business. Instead, you are conducting research, looking for advice or seeking contacts. Most business people do it.

In advance

In terms of planning your specific approach, a phone call is often the best first contact. Prepare your questions carefully. Do not waffle. Make it clear what it is you're asking for. Mention how you came across their name and why you think they would be able to help. Above all, keep it brief.

If the individual you are trying to contact is very senior, it may be difficult or inappropriate to phone. In this case, a short, punchy letter might be a better way of introducing yourself. End the letter by stating that you will follow them up.

The meeting

Frequently, the objective of this initial contact is to arrange a face-to-face meeting. There's no doubt about it, people are generally better in the flesh – you can more easily develop rapport, make eye contact and read their body language. All important factors in leaving a good impression. But many people are nervous about committing their time. So make it clear that you are only asking for a short meeting – half an hour sounds a reasonable investment of their time in you.

Then plan the meeting. How are you going to open it? You should aim to get them talking as quickly as you can. After all, that's what you're there for and most of us prefer talking to listening! Your introduction, therefore, should be brief: who you are and what you're looking for. Don't make them uncomfortable, or put them on the spot with your requests. Don't ask for a job! Don't pose questions that you suspect they won't be able to answer. Make it as easy as you possibly can for them to help you.

Think through the questions you definitely want to ask. Be aware, however, that two basic questions, combined with active listening and intelligent responses to what they say, can easily fill half an hour – or longer! By all means have a checklist of what you'd like to ask: it'll be invaluable if your contact turns out not to be very communicative. But be clear about which are the essential questions, and which are the "nice to haves". One question that is always useful to ask is whether they know of any other people who would be able to help you out.

Make sure you manage the time. Don't use up more time than you've requested. Not, that is, unless *they* seem intent on continuing the debate. Nor should you leave them with actions. It's your project. You should be responsible for the follow-up activity.

Afterwards

After the meeting, write and thank your contact. This is a matter of courtesy and it makes them more inclined to help you out in the future. Perhaps they'd think of introducing you to others. A written reminder certainly means you stay in their minds for longer.

Maintaining your network

Your network will develop and mature over time. People will drop out. Others will fill their shoes. And as your career progresses, the number, range and depth of your relationships with others will grow. But your database of contacts is like a garden: without care and maintenance, the whole thing becomes tangled and unwieldy. The only thing you can do with it is prune heavily and pretty much start again. Consequently, you need to manage and maintain your network.

This means finding a way of being in regular contact with people. And regular means appropriate! For some people, a Christmas card will suffice. With others, you may need to call them monthly to demonstrate your support and interest. Listen carefully to what they have to say and make a note of any developments in their lives. It may be possible to invite them to events – business or otherwise. But you need to be selective. Pareto's law dictates that 80% of the benefit will come from 20% of the contacts. On this basis, there are probably a handful of key people you absolutely have to stay in touch with. Work out who they are and develop a strategy for maintaining your relationship with them. Be careful not to misjudge it: there's nothing worse than becoming a pain in the neck to someone. As the best form of business relationship operates on a "give and take" basis, establish what they're getting out of it, as well as what you want. Think laterally, there may be all sorts of things that you – or other members of your network – can offer them.

Update and review your network diagram regularly. Are there gaps? Are you being sufficiently forward-thinking? Could you usefully introduce some members of your network to others?

As the business world moves away from the notion of using (and abusing) commodity suppliers, and towards working in strategic partnership with carefully selected organizations, you will find yourself high on the list if you have invested time in actively cultivating your network.

CHAPTER 11

Changing the way others see you

> When asked what office politics meant to him, the chief executive of a large public organization responded: "The perception, more often than the reality, that advancements depend less on merit and more on the ability of some individuals to appear more useful and capable than they actually are. People then engage in this type of political activity because they believe it could advance their career, or if they fail, because it will make them feel comfortable with the rejection."

Introduction

A significant development in UK national politics has been the rise of spin-doctors. These are the people charged with building new, improved images of political parties, their policies and their leaders, when the current image is no longer in keeping with the aims of the party. Their role is often two-fold: first they have to eradicate the public's *existing* impression of an individual (if this is perceived to be negative); then they can build a consistent, constructive image which better fits what the party stands for. Spin-doctors exert enormous influence over what politicians do and say – and the *way* in which they do and say it. They consequently have a lot of impact and power in the political world.

Importance of image

In the business world, too, the way in which people are perceived is hugely important. If you consider a job interview, for instance, most interviewers will form an impression of the individual within the first few seconds, and their mind is often made up in two minutes. Of course, more sophisticated interview techniques have been developed to avoid this scenario, ensuring that people are assessed objectively against pre-determined criteria. But without this structured approach, first impressions really can be all important.

Because of this, image consultants are kept very busy, helping people – both male and female – to understand how they should change their clothes/hair/shoes/speech, if they want to be seen as true professionals. Some companies – particularly in the media and consulting sectors – now offer all their staff the opportunity to have a personal consultation. As a result, their personnel are immaculately dressed, groomed and accessorized.

At some point in their lives, most people find themselves in the position of having to change the way others see them. It may be that they want to come across as a more serious player. Or it could be that others have significant negative perceptions which must be shifted if they are going to get on. Many people find out about these views at their annual performance appraisal. Consider the following criticisms:

● You're not confident enough.
● You need to take the initiative more often.
● You're too timid.
● You're too aggressive.
● You don't network enough.
● You're not sufficiently dynamic.
● There's a long way to go before you're ready for promotion.

These are examples of some of the criticisms you could hear at an appraisal interview. The list is by no means exhaustive, but it's illustrative of the type of value judgements made about people. The individuals in question may or (more likely) may not agree with the criticisms. But what can they do about it other than agree or disagree? It's frequently the case that such criticisms are accurate *historically*, but the person has already taken significant steps to address the shortcomings. The feeling of being branded – or not being allowed to improve – can be upsetting and frustrating: "What do I have to *do* to make people recognize that I've changed, that I *can* do it – and what's more, I can do it now?" Time to transform your reputation!

The new you

The process of transformation is not easy, nor is it always speedy. It takes time and requires tenacity. But there is a four-stage model that will help you to bring about a change in your image:

1. Find out what your reputation *really* is.
2. Be clear about what you want it to be.
3. Effect the change.
4. Measure the results.

Find out what your reputation *really* is

There's a lot of talk about the need for feedback on a regular basis and some people are fortunate enough to benefit from this. But in reality, appraisal time is when most people find out what others think about them. And appraisals can be few and far between. So, in the meantime, how should you go about finding out what people really think about you? First, you will have your own views – a gut feeling, based on what you know about yourself, and the way that others treat and respond to you. In a highly political organization, you could also be unlucky enough to have heard bad news about yourself on the grapevine! So start the process by documenting your current impression of what others think of you. Be as honest as you can, listing both the positives and the negatives. Then add evidence to support these comments – recent successes and failures/frustrations.

Get feedback

Once you have done this, it's important to check it out. Ask a couple of people you trust for some feedback. Stress that you want them to be honest and frank with you. If necessary, prompt them by testing out your own perceptions. When they know you are serious about your desire for feedback, they are more likely to start opening up to you. Make sure that you consult a range of people. Include your boss. Maybe seek some comments from customers – ideally, internal *and* external. Then document your summary of the feedback. What are the areas of agreement? Are there subjects on which an individual's view disagrees with your own – or with the others? Why might this be? Once you have completed this analysis, answer the following questions:

- What are my *key* strengths?
- How could these help me in the future?
- What are my *key* weaknesses/areas for development?
- How will these hinder my progress?
- Which elements of the feedback do I consider to be unfair/ unsubstantiated/inaccurate?
- Why?
- What do I feel about all this?

Reflect

Before moving on to stage 2 (being clear about what you want your image to be), reflect on this analysis for a moment. Bear in mind the following:

- It is very important to give some thought to where the feedback comes from. Don't let yourself off the hook, or make a habit of turning a blind eye to all criticisms, but do consider whether ulterior motives could be coming into play in some of the comments made. For instance, an entirely positive view may be driven by the fact that the person giving the feedback values your friendship and wouldn't want to hurt you. The opposite situation could also be true: an overly negative appraisal could be driven by circumstances which are more to do with the other person's feelings and motivations than your performance.
- It is always a good idea to lead from strength and plan for a future based around what you do well. There is a contrary element in all of us that wishes we could be something we're not. But we should play to our strengths. After all, you can teach a turkey to climb a tree, but it's cheaper to hire a squirrel!
- In terms of your areas for development, do you actually *want* to master these skills? Many square pegs are forced into round holes purely because that's the only way to get a promotion. But you do have to demonstrate some interest and aptitude to do a job well. What really interests you?

- Challenge yourself about any seemingly unfair or historical perceptions. Are there things you still do that could give rise to this sort of criticism? If not, why are people saying it?
- Tap into your own feelings. These could be a significant driving force behind actually making the change. Do you really want to feel hurt/depressed/angry, for exactly the same reasons, three months down the line? Don't be tempted into thinking that it doesn't matter what you do, people will always be prejudiced against you. You *can* do something about it. You just need the will power!

Be clear about what you want your image to be

So how do you want to be perceived in your personal Brave New World? Do you want to project a positive, professional image – someone who's going places? Do you want to be seen as an inspirational and caring manager?

Research shows that if you have a clear image of what you want to be in the future, your chances of actually achieving it are much increased. And one way to create this mental picture is to carry out a visualization exercise. If you want to have a go at this, it might make sense to enlist the support of a close friend or colleague. This person will be able to prompt and challenge you, and – at a much more practical level – take notes!

Time frame

First, set an appropriate time frame. Many people find a three-year horizon to be helpful – sufficiently far ahead to be stretching and encourage ambitious thinking, but not so distant that it couldn't inspire action today. If your need to change is more urgent than that, you may wish to reduce the timescale to (say) 18 months. Once you have established this, think about the following questions. In *x* years' time:

- Where will you be living?
- What will your lifestyle be like?
- Where will you be working?
- What sort of job will you be doing?
- How much responsibility will you have?
- What else will be important in your life?

Visualize

Note the answers to these questions, then move onto the visualization exercise itself. First, imagine you have succeeded in achieving all of the above. Close your eyes and summon up a clear mental picture of you in your future world. This may take some time. You may find it difficult to see yourself. Instead you may see things *through your eyes*. Catching a glimpse of yourself in the mirror will then be the only time during the visualization when you see your own image. This is fine. Keeping your eyes closed, and remaining fully relaxed, work through the following questions (this is where having a partner can help you):

- **What does your vision *look* like?** Where are you? Who is in it? What are you doing? What are other people doing? What else can you see around you? Can you describe it?
- **What does your vision *sound* like?** What noises can you hear? What kinds of things are other people saying? What are they saying about you? What are you saying to yourself? What is the general hubbub?
- **What does your vision *feel* like?** How are you feeling? What are your emotions? What are you looking forward to? Looking back, what do you feel about the past three years?

This may be a short exercise, or it could continue for an hour, or longer, during which time your partner (if you have involved one) would be taking notes and prompting you with questions. These should be genuinely open questions (starting with *who, what, where, how, etc.*), rather than closed questions (merely requiring a *yes* or *no* answer) or leading questions (where you turn *your* opinion into a "question" by tacking a "?" onto the end of a statement, or starting off with phrases like "Do you think that…"). Your partner should also be careful to avoid passing comment on, or judging, your vision. "Call that a vision?" or "You don't want to do that" are not helpful comments!

Don't be surprised if, after the first five minutes or so, the visualization becomes very different from your answers to the preliminary questions. Surprises are quite common in this process.

Once you have exhausted all the possibilities, and have created a congruent picture of your future, open your eyes. If you haven't involved anyone else, you may wish to make a note of the key elements – remembering to include how it looks, sounds and feels – while it's still fresh in your mind. Return to this vision regularly. Summon up those same feelings and thoughts. Enjoy the experience. If you do this, your body and mind will subconsciously start to work towards the goals you have set for yourself.

Clearly there will be aspects of your visualization that won't just happen on their own – a move to the other side of the planet, or a complete career change, for instance. But equally, there will be elements that will happen naturally – behaving more confidently, or more positively, for example. Make a point of acting in accordance with your vision: say the right things, wear the right clothes, be the right sort of person.

Effect the change

Most people are quick to make judgements about you – and these first impressions tend to be lasting ones. In addition, they have minds like elephants – you can find one unfortunate slip-up coming back to haunt you years after the event. It's therefore quite difficult to shift another person's impression of you, but not impossible. If you put your mind to it, you can get out of that pigeon hole! There are two aspects to this: action and communication.

So what action are you going to take? We talked above about the almost automatic impact that a strong vision of the future, and a desire to act in accordance with it, can have. But we also alluded to the fact that some elements will need much more concrete planning and action. You need to produce a personal strategy, incorporating your goals, key milestones, how you want others to view you, and the actions required to effect the change.

Personal strategy

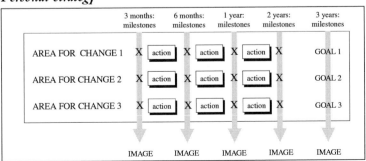

Goals

Take a large sheet of paper and draw the vertical lines indicated in the personal strategy diagram. Refer back to your visualization and list your key goals down the three year line.

Milestones

If you are going to work effectively towards these goals, what **milestones** will you need to hit in three, six, 12 and 24 months' time? For instance, if today you are an accounts clerk, but in three years' time you plan to be a fully-qualified accountant, a key milestone for the three-month mark might be to have contacted the appropriate professional body and registered with them. The six-month milestone might be to have started a correspondence course or attending lectures.

Some of the goals are likely to be less tangible, however. A three-year aim might be to feel entirely confident in your own abilities and comfortable with yourself. A challenging goal! But however intangible, it is essential to break it down into smaller chunks. How *will* that look in six months' time? How *will* you know if you've started to make progress? Be rigorous and specific. Challenge yourself: if I achieve these milestones, will I really be on course for achieving my ultimate aim?

Try to create a milestone for each of the areas for change at each point in time, i.e. the points marked "X" on the personal strategy diagram.

Image

Once your milestones have been incorporated, you need to think about what image you want to project at each of these important stages: how should other people be viewing you? Think about the people who are most important to you, those you need to impress, and those who seem to have a problem with you. What impression should they be left with? Again, be specific. The clearer you are about the image you want to have, the easier it is to plan how you're going to achieve the transition. Note these at the bottom of your personal strategy.

Actions

Then – and only then – should you start to think about planning specific actions, the reason being that actions are more likely to be aligned to goals if you have first given significant thought to what those goals really look like – in the short, medium *and* long term. Actions should be planned in more detail for the first year, and then in skeleton format only for years two and three. Only in exceptional circumstances will it be possible to plan in any detail for the longer term, but you may wish to log important life events, such as starting a family.

It is important to note that actions fall into two categories:

● Actions to help you achieve your goals.
● Actions to convince others that you are changing.

Many people overlook the second aspect, assuming that others will (a) notice the change, (b) believe you mean business, and (c) change their impression of you. That does happen – occasionally. More often, it requires active management, and this is where the communication element comes in.

Measure the results

Go back to the individuals who gave you the feedback in the first place. Explain what you're aiming to do and ask for feedback on how you're doing. Think of ways – either direct or indirect – in which you can reach those people you feel have been gunning for you. Plan how you approach them – you don't want to reinforce any negative impressions. Instead, you want to impress them with the change in you. Six months down the line, repeat the feedback exercise and see how views have changed. But don't leave it to chance – or to others to recognize how the new you is coming along. Make a note of your own successes. Gently blow your own trumpet. And make others recognize that you've changed. It's just as important to get them to accept that the old you is a thing of the past as it is to bring them on board with the new look model.

Above all, remember that this can be a frustrating process. It's difficult enough to change the way you operate, but research shows that it can take up to eight months before other people are prepared to acknowledge the change formally. Whether it's because it takes a while for you to master a new role convincingly, or because they can't believe the evidence of their eyes, or they don't want it to be true, we just don't know. But be patient. And try to avoid confusing "it hasn't happened yet" with "it's not going to happen".

CHAPTER **12**

The manager's guide to managing politics

> An MD in a large retail bank attended a leaving party, where the outgoing executive said: "I knew it was time to go when we started stabbing each other in the front!"

Introduction

How should a *manager* deal with office politics? The most straightforward answer to that question is: "all of the above and more!" Without exception, the issues referred to in previous chapters are relevant for everyone, whatever their position in the organization. Like most other people, managers have conflicts to deal with, they have to exert their powers of influence and persuasion – and they too may have bosses who are difficult to handle!

However, there are some specific problems faced by anyone in a managerial position, and these are covered in this chapter.

Tough at the top

A senior manager in a multinational manufacturing company recently remarked:"If you are a leader, the best you can ever hope for is to break even!" At the time, others considered this to be a cynical remark – isn't leadership more rewarding than that? But as they discussed the issue, it became increasingly clear that the position can be quite an unenviable one.

As a leader, you have to balance a number of seemingly conflicting demands. You are required to set a firm direction – be a charismatic and visionary leader – while constantly consulting people throughout the team. You have to let go of the reins – empower others – while still maintaining an effective understanding of all that's going on in the component parts of your business. You have to coach and give constructive feedback to your team, while you yourself may have access to neither. And throughout, you need to be robust and inspire confidence in others, while being seen to be completely open and honest with people.

What else is new?

This series of balancing acts wouldn't be so bad if you had the luxury of stability. But that's clearly not the case. The environment is changing at a pace the like of which we've never seen before.

As well as this, you're expected to understand, be committed to and effectively implement all the latest management initiatives: matrix management, process management, downsizing, rightsizing and culture change – to name but a few!

We saw in early chapters that a high degree of change – when rules and regulations are open to interpretation and there is greater ambiguity – breeds office politics. In addition, the very nature of some of these management techniques exacerbates the situation. For instance, matrix structures (see example opposite) mean that most people in the organization report to two bosses. This can lead to role ambiguity, conflicting demands and dual accountability.

It also creates the potential for a team member to play one boss off against the other.

Downsizing, or rightsizing as some call it, has led to flatter structures. This reduces the opportunities for traditional career progression, which may lead to greater competition between colleagues – and increased political activity.

Another recent trend, 360° feedback (where your boss, peers

	Manager Product A	Manager Product B	Manager Product C
Manager Europe	Team	Team	Team
Manager America	Team	Team	Team
Manager Asia	Team	Team	Team

Example of a matrix structure. This shows a product/geographical split. Equally, the matrix could be divided by function and project, so that IT specialists, for example, report to a functional IT manager and one or more project managers.

and team input feedback to your appraisal), can give unscrupulous operators an opportunity to stick the knife in, if not planned, and implemented, very carefully.

Whatever the programme of change in your organization, you need to be aware of the potential downside. That doesn't mean to say you have to be suspicious and paranoid! What it does mean is that you need to be on the lookout for any surge in political activity and deal with it constructively.

The tell-tale signs have been well-documented elsewhere. But here is a quick reminder of what you should watch out for in your team:

● Bickering and backstabbing.
● People complaining to you about the behaviour of their colleagues.
● People going outside the department with complaints or unusual requests.
● Rival factions or cliques emerging.

- Hidden agendas.
- Lack of openness in team meetings.
- Lack of co-operation.

It is your responsibility to create a working climate in which people can be open and constructive, and where they can get on with their jobs without the pressure and waste created by a high degree of office politics.

If you do notice any of the symptoms described above – or any of the others outlined in previous chapters – you need to take action.

The critical tasks

One way in which you can view your managerial role is to think in terms of the following five categories. You are responsible for:

- *What* **people are aiming to achieve** – objective setting.
- *How* **they do it** – organizational culture and teamworking.
- **How** *well* **they do it** – effective performance management.
- **What happens when they** *don't* **perform** – addressing poor or inappropriate performance.
- **Walking the talk** – being a good role model for people.

These categories are expanded below.

What people are aiming to achieve

The first question that needs to be asked is: does your team have clear objectives? This may sound like an obvious – and unnecessary – question, but it's remarkable how many people do not have objectives set for them, or do have objectives, but they're vague and woolly. What this means is that people are left to their own devices and – if they are so inclined – are able to pursue their own selfish goals at the expense of others. It may not even be that devious. If people are unclear about what they are supposed to be achieving, they are likely to do what they enjoy doing, or feel comfortable with, rather than what is required for business success.

It is important that people have clear, unambiguous targets to aim for.

Best practice in this area dictates a form of cascade. In other words, when considered collectively, the team's objectives should equal your objectives.

The first thing to do, then, is to examine your own targets. Are they specific and measurable? Are they stretching, but attainable? Are they actually capable of being cascaded? If not, you should seek clarification.

Once your objectives are up to scratch, you then need to apply the same criteria to those of the team. Make sure that timescales are clear. Work with individual team members to agree their objectives – they will have far more commitment to achieving them.

However, it may be that you don't have the luxury of starting from scratch – the team's objectives have already been set, but it seems that people are being forced to compete with one another. In an ideal world, an individual's objectives should be capable of being described as "I win, we all win".

However, it is not uncommon for objectives to be flawed in one of the following ways:

- I win, you lose.
- I win, the team/company loses.
- My team wins, another team loses.

The "I win, you lose" situation used to be rife in the world of sales. Take, for example, a car showroom. One salesperson generated a lead, but they happened to be out of the dealership when the potential customer came in. A second salesperson would leap in, clinch the deal, gain the credit for the sale – and take the commission that goes with it!

The "I win, the team/company loses" situation is where an individual achieves what they need to achieve at the expense of the whole organization. For example, a unit that maximizes its own profitability by getting cheap supplies from outside the group, while another unit – that should be supplying the materials – is crippled with over-capacity and idle machinery. It sounds bizarre, but it's a surprisingly common occurrence.

The third situation – "my team wins, another team loses" – is also widespread. This is where individual teams, who are supposed to work together in order to deliver a product or service, find themselves with apparently conflicting goals – manufacturing vs sales, or systems development vs systems operations – are classic examples.

If you have a problem in this area, what category does your situation fall into? Are the objectives of your own team compatible? Are there areas that are bound to cause conflict or counter-productive behaviour? Or does the problem lie outside? Are there clashes of interest with other teams? On the grounds that *what gets measured, gets done* – a somewhat cynical, but often accurate management philosophy – the way in which people's targets are set up has a significant bearing on the performance and culture of the team. It is important, therefore, to take action to improve the situation.

Sometimes your hands are tied: the way in which objectives are set is dictated by company policy. There is then little you can do, other than lobby senior management, explain the situation to the team and urge them to work constructively around it. However, there is always some scope for action:

- Incorporate an element of team and/or department objectives within an individual's objectives.
- Make sure that people know precisely what their colleagues are trying to achieve.
- Make it clear that you will recognize any efforts to achieve for the greater good, even if that means lower personal performance.
- Explain *your* objectives to the team so that they understand what it is you are trying to achieve through their efforts.

There is a useful tool that managers can employ to create more understanding and co-operation between individuals and teams. This is known as the objectives/support grid (see opposite).

Like many of the best management tools, this one is simple, but produces good, practical results.

Its main purpose is to help people understand what others are trying to achieve and how they will need to support them. They then get the same in return. Ultimately, it could help to facilitate consistency and co-operation throughout an organization.

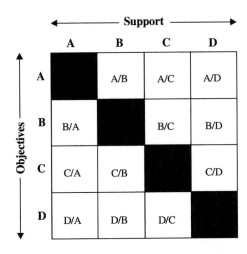

Source: Andrew Forrest, 5 Way Management, The Industrial Society

Use the grid as follows:

- Draw up the grid on a sheet of A3 or flip chart paper.
- Get the people involved around the table (this could be individuals from within a team, or people from different departments).
- Write your name at "A" and your colleagues' names at "B", "C" and "D".
- Summarize your objectives at A/A – headlines only, not the full detail.
- Get your colleagues to follow suit at B/B, C/C and D/D.
- Ask each colleague in turn what they could do to help you achieve your objectives.
- Summarize their responses in the appropriate squares – A/B, A/C and A/D.
- Then move on to each of your colleagues in turn and repeat the exercise.
- Encourage people to listen and participate throughout, especially challenging anything they consider to be impractical or unproductive.

This tool is of most benefit when used to draw out things that are not already happening. It may be expanded to include as many participants as you see fit. Be aware, however, that once you get to 12 people on each axis, the exercise becomes unwieldy and time consuming.

How they do it

It is not sufficient for you to set objectives and allow people to get on with achieving them – in whatever manner they choose. More and more organizations are realizing that behaviours count. Customers will stick with a supplier because they are pleased with the service – often irrespective of a slightly higher price. The best new graduates are becoming more selective about the organizations they join. They want to work in a place that values and develops its people and has an open, positive culture. And what is culture? The way we do things around here. So behaviours *are* important. But those engaged in changing organizational culture will tell you that it's not easy and it takes time.

To minimize destructive office politics in your team, there are two things you need to achieve:

● the right sort of culture
● a teamworking ethos.

Culture

Let's take culture first. How exactly *do* you want people to do things around here? Clarifying this will provide you with a set of your "values". Values have been defined in many ways, but one excellent description is that they are the behaviours observable by the outside world. In other words, the values articulate the personality of the team, the company and the service.

So what does this look like in practice? Well, it could be that you're described as proactive and passionate. Or, maybe you're dedicated to excellent customer service. Or perhaps you're caring and supportive. Whatever the values, they need to be appropriate to the business you're in, of value to the customer, capable of driving behaviour, and realistic. Many organizations go through values exercises and come up with aspirational words that are so far removed from their current situation that the results are laughable. While it's a good idea for the values to be stretching, they shouldn't be so different from the current situation that they lack credibility.

But values are just empty words, unless there is some activity and belief underpinning them. As a manager, you need to communicate the values to all staff. Better still, involve them in helping you to distill them. Give people an opportunity to work out – either in teams, or as individuals – what living the values will mean in their day-to-day activity. Ask them what the barriers are – and what their ideas are for overcoming them. Then reinforce the values – both in terms of what you say, and what you do.

Equally, you should conduct an "audit" of your whole operation. Are the systems, structures, services, products, processes, literature – and people – consistent with the values? For example, if one of your espoused values is "professional" and you don't have one fully-qualified person in your team, then there is a developmental need to address. Make sure that the way you run your business is consistent with the way you are asking people to behave.

It is then important to reward people when they are in line with the values, and address any examples of behaviour which are inconsistent. This is covered in the next three main sections – how *well* they do it, what happens when they *don't,* and walking the talk.

A teamworking ethos

In terms of creating a teamworking ethos, there are a number of criteria you need to ensure are met. Think about your own team and answer the following questions:

	Yes	No
Are your goals clear?		
Are they clearly linked to the business objectives?		
Do you collectively work towards achieving them?		
Do you set realistic timescales?		
Are individuals' roles clear?		
Do you continually review the resources available?		
Are the resources the right ones?		
Does the team have the right mix of skills/styles/experience?		
Is everyone involved who ought to be?		

	Yes	No
Do you communicate effectively and in a timely fashion?		
Do you *want* to achieve the goals?		
Do you have good team meetings?		
Do you recognize the value of others?		
Does everyone contribute to the team?		
Do you respect the right of people to have different views?		
Do you give support?		
Do you feel supported?		
Do you build on ideas and share values?		
Do you learn from experience?		
Are you honest with each other?		
Do you hold regular performance reviews?		
Are development plans in place?		
Do you provide regular feedback?		
Is feedback constructive?		
Do you celebrate successes?		

The more ticks you are honestly able to put in the "yes" column, the stronger teamworking is likely to be in your area. Each "no" answer brings with it the potential for a serious problem – perhaps related to how well you are likely to achieve the task, or having a negative impact on the people involved. But in the spirit of teamworking, it's not right for you to be judge and jury on this issue. *You* may think that things are fine and dandy, but other team members could have quite a different view. Get them together and go through the questions as a group. Without being defensive, explore what they are saying:

- Why do you say that?
- Is it a widespread issue?
- When does it tend to happen?
- What are our biggest problems?
- What can we do to address them?
- Who is going to do what?
- By when?
- What will be our measures of success?

This type of team exercise is useful, not only in providing answers to questions, but also in terms of opening up communications.

People will gradually become more used to voicing their opinions, instead of keeping them bottled up or complaining in private with a co-conspirator.

How *well* they do it

Once you have established what people should be delivering – and how they should do it – it is important to ensure that things stay on track and that people know how *well* they are performing. You need to give day-to-day feedback – praising progress and successes, and constructively criticizing when people are not meeting your requirements. In addition, you must make sure that the performance management or appraisal process is in line with how you want people to behave.

Longnecker, Sims and Gioia conducted a study of 60 senior executives – with experience of appraising people in almost 200 companies – and concluded that political considerations are almost always part of the performance evaluation process. The appraisors were less concerned about the accuracy of their feedback than the impact it had on the individual. Feedback was more positive when the individual being appraised was a person with whom the manager had a good relationship and wanted to motivate. And the reasons? Well, first and foremost, those involved in the study justified their behaviour on the grounds that it is a manager's prerogative to exercise discretion in these matters. Since appraisals can have a considerable impact on an individual's career, and involves a written document, they believed it important to give a glowing account of people with potential.

This is human nature. We all have personal biases and preferences. But these findings throw a disturbing light on the objectivity of the performance appraisal process.

This is not a straightforward issue, since some of the negative feelings you have about an individual could be held by others – and could indeed get in the way of good performance. Similarly, what you like about an individual – your bias – could be a significant factor in their ability to work well across departmental boundaries. So the first thing to do is to challenge your personal opinion:

● What exactly do/don't I like about this individual?
● Is that fair?

- If yes, *why* do I say it's fair?
- Do others feel the same way?
- What is the impact?

Once you have clarified your thinking in this way, you will have a clear idea of whether it is right and relevant to incorporate the view in the appraisal. If you do still think it appropriate to mention, these personal considerations need to be separated out from the performance issues. Again, it's human nature to think of an individual as a good performer, when actually you just like and admire them. Make sure that your performance criteria are as objective as they possibly can be and give sound, well thought-through feedback across all dimensions.

What happens when they *don't* perform

One sure-fire way to ensure that office politics is rife in your team is to allow certain individuals to continue behaving in a way that is at odds with your espoused culture – and do absolutely nothing about it. Trying to instigate a positive change in your area, but then turning a blind eye to dissenters, has a far greater negative impact than adopting a laissez-faire attitude in the first place. Those who have tried become disillusioned and cynical, and those who haven't feel they've won some sort of victory for the old regime. You need to let people know that you mean business by cracking down on unacceptable behaviour.

How to deal with this type of situation is well documented in Chapter 5. If you have a problem in this area, recognize it and then take action!

Walking the talk

Most managers are surprised when confronted with the impact they have on the team. Every word they utter is passed on and interpreted – often not in a wholly constructive way. Every behaviour seems to have hidden meaning. When they get something wrong, the ripples – and remonstrations – are phenomenal. It's not surprising, therefore, to find that managers "paying lip service" is one of the reasons most frequently cited for the failure of change programmes. The manager may have set sound objectives, made it clear how they want people to behave, and then rewarded good performance and dealt with bad. But if they then behave in a way that is inconsistent with what they are saying, it's likely to undo all the good work.

As a manager, therefore, role modelling is an essential skill. And what is it? It's all about behaviour, since that's the only thing that people can judge you on. It doesn't matter about your good intentions, or your inner feelings, if your actions let you down.

You need to get the balance right between opening up and presenting a confident, reliable front. You must think through the potential implications of an action – *before you act* – and ensure that the way you do it sets the best possible example. If you do slip up, it's remarkable how much credit you will get for admitting your mistake to the team, and assuring them it won't happen again. But don't do it too often. You – like everybody else – are supposed to be learning from your mistakes, not frequently repeating them in the knowledge that confession will earn you a pardon!

Making it count

By taking action on these five fronts – goal setting, establishing a culture of openness and teamwork, managing performance, addressing poor performance, and acting as a role model – you will bring about positive change. By constantly reviewing how well you are doing, and taking corrective action if you are going off course, you will make sure that the change is not a one-off, but an integral part of the way you do business.

Office politics will still rear its head, but any destructive activity will be nipped in the bud, and you will have a team that is influential, powerful and satisfied – not manipulative and devious.

Epilogue

This book has been based on three core assumptions:

1. Some political activity is inevitable in all organizations.
2. Office politics can be destructive, but appropriately motivated political activity facilitates the smooth running of an organization and can do so in a way which benefits most people who work in it.
3. It is, therefore, desirable that everyone belonging to a particular organization understands how political forces operate within it, although they may choose not to become actively involved in political activity themselves.

Some organizations are certainly more political than others, while the motivation of *office politicians* varies enormously. At one extreme, you can observe an almost saintly concern for the common goal; at the other, you find the relentless pursuit of self-interest and personal aggrandisement.

What I have tried to do is help you recognize some of the most common ploys used in office politics and, where appropriate, to outline some strategies which can help you protect your legitimate rights and personal interests, when these seem to be under threat.

Of course, some people will still choose to follow the Canute option, protesting loudly that an organization can function without political activity, or that if it can't, then it ought to be able to. Unfortunately, people who do so are no more likely to find organizational life comfortable than the king was to keep his feet dry!

If you do decide to take an active part in the political dimension of office life, you may do so either to overcome obstacles or rectify problems caused by other people's politicking, or, more positively, to influence events in a fashion which suits your own purposes. Of course, these may very well coincide with those of the organization as a whole, and you should be able to push them forward without disadvantaging anyone else (which is a vital consideration).

Almost irrespective of the nature of the situation, the scale of the problem and the people involved, there are three basic steps that will help you to achieve what you need to achieve. They are:

- analyse accurately the dynamics of the situation
- assess swiftly the motivation of the other people involved
- act effectively to achieve an outcome which is to the benefit of the organization as a whole, ideally by creating a win-win situation.

But, whatever the depth or the motivation of your practical involvement in the process, I hope that your overall perception of office politics is now one of confident understanding, rather than anxious bafflement.